COMPARATIVE PERSPECTIVES
ON
INDIAN LITERATURE

COMPARATIVE PERSPECTIVES

ON

INDIAN LITERATURE

Edited by

A. RAMAKRISHNA RAO

Professor of English

Sri Krishnadevaraya University

PRESTIGE

Published by
Prestige Books
3/28, East Patel Nagar, New Delhi 110 008
in association with
Indian Society for Commonwealth Studies
New Delhi

ISBN 81-85218-64-1

Phototypesetting by
Laser Impressions
New Delhi 110 028
Ph. 537756, 537296

Printed at
Mehra Offset Press
New Delhi 110 002

Contents

Preface

In most of our universities, Indian Literature is offered as an optional paper. This suggests that the concept of Indian Literature is not a reformist cry, but an academic reality. Given the multiplicity of languages in which Indian Literature is accessible, one is forced to be cautious in describing its characteristic features, let alone defining them. A comparative assessment of Indian literature may proceed in terms of its regional and linguistic variety. It is not unity but difference that characterises Indian Literature. But sometimes it is necessary and meaningful to evaluate Indian Literature by comparing it with the literatures of other countries and cultures.

Prof. S. Viswanathan's "Cultural Factors in Comparative Studies" offers a mature statement of some of the ways in which a comparative study of Indian Literature may proceed. While Prof. M. Sivaramakrishna cogently argues that a critical formula, if not a poetics, could be evolved from the traditional Indian concepts, "Sruti/Smriti," Prof. Raghavacharyulu's critique of Sri Aurobindo's *Savitri* exemplifies the way in which Western poetics could be applied in interpreting an Indian text. G.R. Taneja's article on Dinkar's *Urvashi* makes a welcome contribution to comparative Indian literature.

Going a step further, Dr. P. Ramachandraiah vigorously argues that the Jamesian canons of creative and critical methods are sometimes inapplicable in interpreting a Telugu text like *Ekaveera*. Without resorting to a theory like "the anxiety of influence," Prof. C.D. Narasimhaiah clarifies the Gandhian ethic and its dynamic assimilation and transformation of very significant western ideals. Dr. S. Ramaswamy and Dr. Makarand Paranjape focus their attention on Raja Rao's texts in order to specify some of the interpretive problems they pose to a reader. Although their critical approaches are different, they seem to agree on Raja Rao's stature as a novelist. Prof. C. Subba

Rao and Dr. Prema Nandakumar give a comparative touch to their assessment of Indian poetry in English.

By and large the contributors to this volume appear to be interested in a comparative discussion of a literature which has a rich potential in terms of human values and cultural nationalism. But whether it is useful in the larger context to evolve an Indian poetics and adhere to notions of Indian sensibility or to develop Comparative poetics to negotiate not only with cultural nationalism but with cultural cross-fertilization is an open question and requires very formidable historical and critical effort.

The editor feels that the labour involved in bringing out this *festschrift* is a labour of love. The respect and esteem he has for Sri R.A. Jayantha defies articulation. He is extremely grateful to all the contributors for their scholarly contributions. He places on record his sincere obligation to Dr. C.R. Visweswara Rao for his help and advice in completing this enterprise. He is also indebted to Dr V.V.N. Rajendra Prasad for his help at a time when it was much needed. Dr P. Ramachandraiah and Mr K. Selvan have provided the necessary material and moral support in pushing this labour of love through to its successful conclusion. The editor has nothing to offer them but his humble gratitude. Also, I appreciate the suggestions made by Dr. R.K. Dhawan at various stages in the preparation of this project. Finally, thanks are due to Prestige Books, New Delhi, for their prompt decision to publish this volume. I only hope that the book will be of interest both to the scholars and the general students of Indian Literature.

Sri R.A. Jayantha

I am happy to write this brief note on Sri Jayantha for the Festschrift to be presented to him to mark his sixtieth birthday and his retirement from a long and distinguished service in the Department of English of Sri Venkateswara University, Tirupati. Permit me to state that writing as I do as a friend and colleague of Jayantha of long standing, what I say is impersonal and objective enough.

Easily one of the most respected and valued academics on the University scene, he has the credit of having won the minds and hearts of successive batches, indeed, at least of two generations of students and colleagues. His whole approach to teaching, classroom lectures and discussions and tutorial and research guidance and to his personal research and scholarship, has been based on sound instincts and well cultivated habits of scholarship and literary response, of effective communication and intersubjective relations, all of which provide a model for emulation. No wonder that many students of his gratefully remember how his teaching brought to them not only an experience of literature but the habit of an experience of literature.

His literary-critical perceptiveness and capacity to share it with his students and readers of his many published papers of quality and his scholarly scrupulosity bear testimony to the happy blend of heredity and individual talent he could achieve. Worthy son that he is of his illustrious father Sri Rallapalli Ananthakrishna Sarma, he has refined and reapplied his sensibility and intellect in the field of English literary and related studies. His response to problems of translation, of Telugu literature and of music has been fruitful of insights. His essays on Gerard Manley Hopkins and on Indo-English Literature are very highly regarded.

One phase of his career is now complete; his record of service is unique in that his impressive innings has been compiled in one university on the holy soil of Tirupati. Yet, 'the best is yet to be' in his case. His literary-critical activity and his cultural studies will, we may be sure, continue to flourish. Let us heartily wish him many more years of happy and peaceful family and individual life, good health and intellectual and cultural activity.

(Professor) S. VISWANATHAN
University of Hyderabad
Hyderabad

Sri R.A. Jayantha

Long time friend and erstwhile colleague, I could hardly write of Mr. Jayantha without being a bit personal. Our daily association as colleagues lasted for over seven years when there was ample time for the usual academic bickerings. But there was absolutely nothing I could recall about which we should be ashamed of ourselves. It was a long moment of literary naivete: one day you could be reading a poem, another day discussing a critical article or listening to music, or on an odd day going on a picnic all the while learning to live life with no better aid or equipment than a set of texts which we thought, quite innocently, would redeem the world.

Mr. Jayantha's is the sort of sensibility which is easier to recognise than to define. He appears to me as one who has always been less than fair to himself both in terms of what he could do and what he has actually done. Unassuming and modest to a fault, he gave a refreshingly warm response to whatever is creatively good. He affected a distaste for literary theory all the while carrying it without his knowledge. He was very meticulous and thorough in his preparation for any class which he was teaching. He wrote a very neat and beautiful hand, as beautiful as he was handsome. He was never angry but he could be indignant on an occasion when the matter related to any moral purpose. His innate love for melody and music enabled him to cultivate an exquisite sense for the magic of poetry. He looked upon teaching more as a vocation than as a mere profession.

(Professor) C. SUBBA RAO
Andhra Pradesh Open University
Hyderabad

Contributors

S. Laxmana Murthy is Professor of English at Kakatiya University, Warangal.

Prema Nandakumar is a free-lance writer based at Srirangam, Tamilnadu.

C.D. Narasimhaiah is Director, "Dhvanyaloka," Centre for Commonwealth Studies, Mysore.

Makarand Paranjape is Reader in English at the University of Hyderabad, Hyderabad.

D.V.K. Raghavacharyulu is Professor Emeritus at Nagarjuna University, Nagarjuna Nagar.

P. Ramachandraiah is Reader in English at Sri Venkateswara University, Tirupati.

A. Ramakrishna Rao is Professor of English at Sri Krishnadevaraya University, Anantapur.

S. Ramaswamy is Reader in English at Bangalore University, Bangalore.

C. Subba Rao is Professor of English at Andhra Pradesh Open University, Hyderabad.

M. Sivaramakrishna is Professor of English at Osmania University, Hyderabad.

G.R. Taneja is Reader in English at R.L.A. College, University of Delhi, New Delhi.

S. Viswanathan is Professor of English at the University of Hyderabad, Hyderabad.

Crosscultural Factors in Comparative Studies: Some Reflections on Cases in Point

S. VISWANATHAN

Fluellen: Kill the poys and the luggage! 'Tis expressly against the law of arms. 'Tis as arrant a piece of Knavery, mark you now, as can be offert; in your conscience, now, is it not?

Gower: 'Tis certain there's not a boy left alive, and the cowardly rascals that ran from the battle ha' done this slaughter. Besides, they have burn'd and carried away all that was in the King's tent; wherefore the King, most worthily, hath caus'd every soldier to cut his prisoner's throat. O, 'tis a gallant King!

Fluellen: Ay, he was born at Monmouth, Captain Gower. What call you the town's name where Alexander the Pig was born?

Gower: Alexander the Great.

Fluellen: Why? I pray you, is not "pig" great? The pig, or the great, or the mighty, or the huge, or the magnanimous, are all one reckonings, save the phrase is a little variations.

Gower: I think Alexander the Great was born in Macedon. His father was called Philip of Macedon, as I take it.

Fluellen: I think it is in Macedon where Alexander is porn. I tell you, captain, if you look in the maps of the orld, I warrant you sall find, in the comparisons between Macedon and Monmouth, that the situations, look you, is both alike. There is a river in Macedon, and there is also moreover a river at Monmouth. It is call'd Wye at Monmouth; but it is out of my prains what is the name of the other river; but 'tis all one, 'tis alike as my fingers is to my fingers, and there is salmons in both. If you mark Alexander's life well, Harry of Monmouth's life is come after it indifferent well, for there is figures in all things. Alexander, God knows, and you know, in his rages; and his furies, and his wraths, and his cholers, and his moods, and his displeasures, and his indignations, and also being a little intoxicates in his prains, did, in his ales and his angers, look you, kill his best friend, Clytus.

Gower: Our King is not like him in that; he never kill'd any of his friends.

Fluellen: It is not well done, mark you now, to take the tales out of my mouth, ere it is made and finished. I speak but in the figures and comparisons of it: as Alexander kill'd his friend Clytus, being in his ales and his cups; so also Harry Monmouth, being in his right wits and his good judgments, turn'd away the fat knight with the great belly doublet. He was full of jests, and gipes, and knaveries, and mocks – I have forgot his name.

Gower: Sir John Falstaff.

Fluellen: That is he. I'll tell you there is good men porn at Monmouth.

Shakespeare, *King Henry V* (IV, vii, 1 51)
Quotation from *The Riverside Shakespeare*

Such are the excesses perpetrated by that pioneer comparatist, Captain Fluellen of *King Henry V*, the Welshman whom Shakespeare treats most kindly of all his Welsh characters but yet whom the playwright endows with an obsessive over-enthusiasm for the comparative. The Fluellen example should serve as an *exemplum ad horrendum* of how *not* to draw comparisons, and as a warning against 'salmons-in-both' kind of arguments from the comparative. But, unfortunately, in spite of the by now considerably long evolution of comparative literary studies, we tend to lapse at times almost unawares into would-be findings in the Fluellen mode in our exercises in comparison. Worse, sometimes we go on from that to speculate about, or even postulate, connections and influences, against the canons of probability or for that matter historical possibility.

True, thanks to the modernist and postmodern trend of increasing cosmopolitanism and thanks to the influence of Jungian ideas of the collective unconscious, of myth and archetypes, modified yet corroborated by the Fryean ideas, ample warrant would seem to be available for tracing common ground among features and phenomena of works of literature far divided in time and space. We sometimes wonder whether it is not high time that we abandon the age-old habit of the nationalism marking of literatures and start thinking in terms of Literature or World Literature. We also wonder if we as students of English Literature (whether we understand the term as British Literature or, liberally, as British, American, Indo-English and other Commonwealth Literature) are not, inevitably, by virtue of our cultural, linguistic and national positioning, obliged to look at and respond to what we study from a sort of comparative angle. The comparison, often implicit and covert, and sometimes brought into the realm of the overt and the explicit, is with examples, with differing degrees and kinds of relevance, of our own literatures. All the same, it is desirable and necessary in these cases to remind ourselves that the comparative by its very definition includes, transcend as it may, the contrastive. Truly discriminating attention to the element of unlikeness and difference is a critical modicum and desideratum. The true cross-illumination which more than any one-way illumination of a particular text that literary comparison may provide should be the richer advantage of comparative study has a greater chance of being achieved if the differences in sociocultural orientation and the cultural nuances instead of being ignored or obliterated or smoothed over are given due weight.

We may try to understand this particular kind of problem in comparative study, with reference to some three or so cases in point.

We shall start with a relatively simple example. In *The Anglo-Saxon Chronicles*, the annals for 755 A.D. carry an account of the fights between two chieftains Cynewulf and Cyneheard. This extract from the chronicles has been much anthologized and has invariably been among the selections from Old English readers prescribed for study. In the spare, stark prose of the extract is reported the play of the fell, incensed points of the mighty opposites, the two chieftains. In a bitter final confrontation there takes place a real fight to the finish, at the end of which, somewhat as at the end of a fight, which Coleridge speaks of, between two cats only part of a cat's tail is left, the sole survivor is a single badly-wounded person among many fighters on either side. The chieftain in exile with a handful of his followers is surprised by the enemy force in his retreat inside a hall and bower. Thus challenged, he and his companions readily take up arms as though against the sea. The enemies announce that they are prepared to let their kinsmen have a safe passage out if they were to be willing to leave the side of the besieged chieftain. But the followers of the besieged chieftain very promptly and without the slightest hesitation reject the offer and declare that they would not leave their chieftain for fear of fighting against their kinsmen on the enemy side exactly as their kinsmen earlier on did not ever entertain the idea of leaving their master in order to avoid the delicacy and embarrassment of fighting against their kinsfolk on the opposite side. A fight then ensues and results in mutual annihilation.

The narrative in the Chronicles implicitly emphasises the Anglo-Saxon and Germanic code of warrior-heroism and of loyalty to one's master and chief according to which latter ideal, so to say, if blood is thicker than water, loyalty is thicker than blood. The paradigm of the episode invites comparison with the situation at the opening of the *Bhagavad Gita* in terms of the question of the conflict between warrior-like duty and the ties of kinship. It appears as though it is not for the Anglo-Saxon warriors to be in the kind of doubt and dilemma Arjuna was in. Does it mean that they stood in no need of a Krishna and his *Gitaupadesa*? Can we say that they could fare forward on the path of heroic duty because they knew Krishna's philosophy by instinct? Or can we swerve to the other extreme and simply argue that the Anglo-Saxon episode represents a blind following of a primitive animal heroism whereas the *Gita*'s opening situation presents a much more highly evolved and much more sensitive human dilemma on the part of Arjuna?

The generic differences between chronicle annals and a philosphical-poem-inset in the *Mahabharata* epic apart, Arjuna has a self-conscious recognition, at the very moment of his engagement, of the problem of mutual violence between brothers and kinsmen (a recognition which includes an apprehension of the potential brotherly violence has for causing cultural disintegration, an insight which governs René Girard's *Violence and the Sacred*). Such a perception is totally alien to, and not within the ken of the Anglo-Saxon warrior or annalist. This is not to say that the Anglo-Saxon civilization or literature or way of life was primitive in the pejorative sense. The conventions and codes which governed Anglo-Saxon life, literature and art were too elaborately constructed ones for that. In the 755 annals the question is consciously posed whether kinsman should fight and kill kinsman for the raiders do offer to allow their kinsmen among the besieged safe passage and those kinsmen refuse the offer pointing out in the process that their kinsmen on the opposite side had fought against their kith and kin in their staunch battle loyalty and that the besieged men's attitude could not be different. The question is, after all, thus raised and answered in terms of a clear-cut choice of loyalty over blood-relationship, declared and demonstrated in lurid fashion. The value system governing the Anglo-Saxon episode has its similarities with the value system which informs the *Gita* discourse. But the probing and the deeply experiential rethinking of his conduct and of the values of life guiding it which Arjuna consciously undertakes and in which exploration courses are charted for him as a divine gift by Krishna are far beyond the scope of the Anglo-Saxon example which is one of an immediate acceptance and celebratory lustration of the values of loyal heroism.

Arjuna's dilemma would seem to provide a point of reference to what may well be called the most famous dilemma in English literature, that of Hamlet. It has been suggested that both the heroes Arjuna and Hamlet are caught in a similar inner conflict over the question to act or not to act, over the choice between the concept of honour as inward consistency with one's own nature and values and the concept of honour as an external display and public demonstration of physical valour, as, for example, by Alur Janakiram, "Arjuna and Hamlet. Two Moral Dilemmas," *Philosophy East and West* (Hawaii, 1968) (also S. Ramaswamy, "Hamlet and Vedanta" and Sitaram Ramaswamy, "The Shakespeare Upanishad," both in *The Indian Journal of Shakespeare Studies*, 1986). But the really fruitful correspondences to look for are in the respective addresses of Arjuna and Hamlet to their predicaments as much as in their predicaments themselves. And the correspondences consist in contrasts and parallelisms alike.

The state of mind and the consciousness which Hamlet represents are marked by a *Weltschmerz* and an attitude of recoil and near-disgust which qualities at least for the moment overwhelm Arjuna's consciousness just before the start of the battle. The factors which are behind such an attitude are very different in the two cases. Yet both Arjuna and Hamlet can be seen as caught in the process of facing and undergoing a crisis in values. In both cases, the crisis of the particular person acquires large general dimensions. These larger implications make themselves in evidence when we relate *Hamlet* by virtue of its positioning in history to changing world-views and to shifts in consciousness. Similarly, in terms of Krishna's response to and resolution of Arjuna's particular case takes on the proportions of the divine enlightenment of the ideas of human nature, human duty, non-attached engagement in life and the relationship between the human person and a personal God; the *Gita* thus acquires its historic status or rather the status of an intersection between time and eternity.

The contexts of the situations of the two crisis-ridden figures differentiate themselves in several ways. The givens of Hamlet's situation like his father's death, the hasty remarriage of his recently widowed mother, the Ghost's revelation and command with its ambivalent provisos are not exactly shared by Arjuna in his predicament. Yet in his experience, and in his formulation, of his dilemma, Arjuna exhibits the same feeling and stance of an enervation, of slackening of the will and something like a suspension of the sense of duty. Arjuna in his dejection feels a sense of grief and a kind of death-wish much like Hamlet. Arjuna has a fear of the defilement of the family which war and its affirmation would bring about in a way similar to Hamlet's sense of the corrupted state of himself, his family and kingdom if not the world at large. But, clearly, Hamlet has hardly anything like the readily available source of counsel and exhortation which Arjuna has. Horatio, for all Hamlet's eulogy about him, or for that matter the Ghost, is not equivalent of Krishna. The similarity in the dilemmas of Arjuna and Hamlet is but a point of departure; Arjuna's internalizing of his predicament and problem in Chapter I of the *Gita* is, after all, a brief initial phase. The 'dialogue of the mind with itself' which Arjuna is in during this phase soon yields place to Krishna's discourse, whatever dialogic features may mark this apparent monologue. There are, of course, the basic differences in conception and presentation of character, situation and idea between the theatre medium of tragic drama and the meditative poem. The multi-dimensional oral-visual stage-realization and communication, and the polyphonic design and movement of a play with action, acting and actions can create impressions of complexities and intensities different from those of a philosophical poem. The poem, contextualized in the immediacy of an actual theatre of war, draws upon its mode of direct communication, of ideological enunciation and of unmediated manipulation of response.

Hamlet has to work out his salvation (quite a few of the large number of unfavourable critics of Hamlet would say 'damnation') practically on his own. One way of looking at the evolution of Hamlet in the play is to consider him as a figure who comes to embody in himself the paradox of action in inaction and inaction in action, the ideal postulated by Krishna in the *Gita*, and as a figure who increasingly recognizes the paradox of an intermingling of art and life, of life and death. He explores and exploits the paradoxical interrunning into each other of art and actual life in the Mousetrap scene and of a similar collapsing together of performance and reality, jest and earnest and wit and seriousness almost throughout the play. On return from his sea voyage, Hamlet comes to see the paradox of life and death in full and thus comes to accept the challenges of both alike. Thus, in some sense, can be seen in *Hamlet* a semblance of an enactment of certain ideals outlined in the *Gita*. It is Matthew Arnold's insufficient recognition of the paradox of action in inaction and inaction in action, a central idea of the *Gita*, in spite of his well documented and well canvassed acquaintance with the work, that led him to express his preference for the poetry of action and his dissatisfaction with the 'dialogue of the mind with itself' such as *Hamlet* represents in his Preface to the 1853 *Poems*. (It should be added, however, that in his later poetry and cultural criticism Arnold does acknowledge and celebrate the ideal.)

An area of comparative studies which would seem worth investigating but has not elicited much attention so far is the allegorical drama of the late Middle Ages in English and in Sanskrit. It was during this period that allegorical drama was a flourishing tradition in the form of the moralities and slightly later the Interludes in English, and allegorical drama was being written in Sanskrit and possibly performed. Whereas the allegorical morality drama marks the early phase of a thriving and fruitful tradition of drama in England, the allegorical drama in Sanskrit signifies practically the decline and decadence if not the end of Sanskrit theatre as a live institution. This mode in Sanskrit drama may be said to have been inaugurated by Krishnamisra's *Prabhodachandrodayam* of the eleventh century, and a major example of the genre is Vedantadesika's rejoinder of a play entitled *Sankalpasuryodaya* of the twelfth century. Krishnamisra's play is a religious allegory, and an allegory promoting the Advaita religion, while Vedantadesika's rebuttal holds up the cause of Vishishtadvaita. This phenomenon of the use of allegorical drama for religious controversy was to mark the period of the Reformation in England. Krishnamisra's play depicts the protagonist, a king of Benares named Mahamoha, misled by his companions a set of Faults and Vices with whom the king wallows in ignorance and cheap luxury after having banished the good counsellors Religion and Reason. In time Faith and Wisdom come forward to save the king and redeem him from evil. Vedantadesika's play portrays the greater power of Bhakti and surrender of the human to the divine. But despite the great doctrinal force and importance of these plays, and the interest of the debate element in these and subsequent allegorical plays in Sanskrit like Yasahpala's *Mahaparajaya* (14th century), and still later, Ānandārayamakhin's *Vidyaparinaya* (18th century—it bears resemblance to the sixteenth-century English morality, *The Marriage of Wit and Science*), the plays fail to take real dramatic life mainly because the allegory does not come alive for the most part. The characters are very much at the level of mere personification; they are abstractions simply labelled as figures. The abstract concepts of inward qualities, of the mental phenomena, and of virtues and vices, fail to be visualised as particular concretenesses. This sort of an apprehension of the abstract as the concrete could take place in the best, really live examples of morality drama in English as, for instance, *Mankind* and *The Castle of Perseverance* (rather than *Everyman*), thanks to there being produced a popular cultural climate and a popular cultural tradition which included an allegorical habit of mind and of vision that enabled one to see, inwardly and instinctively, of course, an abstract concept as a concrete figure. Such envisioning marked the allegorical tradition in poetry and drama, as well as in popular pageants and processions, at its best, as, for example, in the poetry of Langland and of Dante.

It is not as though there was no strong allegorical tradition in Sanskrit. The interpreters and commentators over the centuries if anything tend to have too much of a penchant for allegorizing. But when it comes to drama even in the best instances of allegorical drama the Sanskrit dramatist works on the abstract level of ideas, and handles allegory as no more than a mode of expression, not as a mode of conception and active apprehension, let alone employing anything like the faculty of the allegorical visualizing of the abstract as a concreteness. The main reasons why the Sanskrit allegorical playwright does not quite succeed are not far to seek. The Indian allegorical tradition, quite in contrast to the Indian tradition of art and drama, poetry and literature, does not seem to have ever achieved the interfusion with our composite of rich popular cultural traditions. This apart, the allegorical drama of Krishnamisra and Vedantadesika situates itself very much in the learned if not the courtly tradition, and for reasons of a certain cultural cleavage fails to inherit the spirit of a more or less homogenizing unification of the learned and the popular which its forbears like Kalidasa, Bhasa, Visakhadatta and, most of all, Sudraka (in his *Mric-cha-katika*) and Rajasekhara (in his Prakrit *Karpuramanjari*) were able to achieve all but spontaneously on account of their participation in a prevailing unity of sensibility in their sociocultural ethos. *Prab-hodachandrodayam* was a much translated play with a Telugu translation in the fourteenth-fifteenth century, a Hindi translation in the seventeenth century with Punjabi and Bengali translations to follow soon after. The play has its crude witticisms about the hypocritical double lives of the Benares Brahmins as well as Buddhist and Jain monks. But, evidently the translations were made not because of the play's dramatic merit, but because the doctrinal preaching and the crude humour lent themselves to translation and to use with a wide audience. The humour is one of refined coarseness and has not much to do with popular culture despite the scenes of gambling and drinking.

Furthermore, what would seem to be taking place in Sanskrit allegorical drama is an attempt deliberately to make drama religious. It is indeed the deliberateness of the venture which would seem to cause or at any rate to entail a certain cultural dichotomizing. The development of drama in late medieval England has in the more recent years been reunderstood as a divergent rather than as a continuous, evolutionary growth, as it earlier used to be considered from church ritual and church drama, by scholars like V.A. Kolve and Glynne Wickham. Morality drama has now been shown to be a distinct and simultaneously emerging phenomenon alongside the mystery plays and not an evolutionary offshoot of these as E.K. Chambers, Karl Young and Hardin Craig made it out to be earlier in the century. Moreover, as Glynne Wickham and others have suggested, the mystery drama partakes of many features, and drives and urges, of popular life, culture and consciousness for all its being probably written by members of the learned clergy. In a parallel development in theories about the origins of European and Greek drama, the view of the ritual origins of drama put forward by the 'Cambridge school of anthropologists', Jane Ellen Harrison, F.M. Cornford and Gilbert Murray has been challenged by William Ridgeway, A.W. Pickard-Cambridge and H.D.F. Kitto, the general thrust of their argument being that the emergence, and growth, of drama is rather to do with popular games, song and dance and popular festive observances and celebrations. In a further parallel development, the play element in cultural manifestations has been emphasized from different points of view by Johan Huizinga and Roger Callois; we may also note in this connection the views about the role of festive indulgence in the development of drama put forward by C.L. Barber and Mikhail Bakhtin's ideas about the central role of carnival in culture and art.

These emphases or rather these recent shifts of emphasis only serve to confirm our impression that drama, in its process of becoming a vigorous major sociocultural form and institution, develops in a pattern of divergent growth from religion which it uses as a point of departure even as it may incorporate the religious element in itself as in Italy and France. What happens in Sanskrit allegorical drama with its designed religionism in the medieval period would seem to be the reverse of the process of the growth of English drama at about the same period of history. For all its polemical vigour and devotional force, the allegorical drama of Krishnamisra and Vedantadesika does not succeed as drama, for the gift of imaging the idea as a concrete particularity which Vedantadesika in his religious experience and thought as a great Vaishnavite possessed in abundant measure in respect of his apprehending the idol worshipped by him as God himself, and not as a mere sign of the Godhead could not carry through into his dramatic imagination. If the faculty failed to operate at the level of his dramatic conception and execution, the explanation why is perhaps to be sought in the severance of the drama from the popular imagination, and the concomitant denial of popular interest and appeal to the religious content of the drama. The use of allegory in this drama could not rise above the level of an exercise in abstraction as it could not in any case derive strength or support from the popular cultural climate which itself for whatever reasons did not nurse or promote the habit of active allegorical visualization. Nor could this drama in any way help to bring about the habit. It is hardly surprising, then, that *Mattavilasa* a Sanskrit play which is imbued with vigour and theatrical life is one which far from being a contribution to religious controversy is a satire on religious controversies and sectarianisms and on the *odium theologicum*.

The foregoing is a pointer in brief to some of the issues posed by the crosscultural complications inherent in the comparative study of texts and genres of two or more different literatures and nations whether they are distanced in time or space or both. This short essay has not undertaken to attempt any full scale analysis of texts set side by side from a comparative angle. It has no more than tried to outline a few issues of a crosscultural nature insofar as these impinge on the comparison of texts and modes. As we know, the possibilities and openings for work in comparative studies with western and eastern classics are tremendous, and manifold are the opportunities for comparative poetics and for cross-illumination of theories, ancient and modern and postmodern of the west and the east. There is also the vast field of the relations of English literature to eastern myth, legend, history and literatures, as well as there being the equally vast area of study of the impact of English literature on eastern literatures, life and thought. In all these expanding fields of study, the more careful and the more searching the attention we pay to cultural variations and qualitative differences of the cultural climates involved, the more rewarding are likely to be the results of our study.

By way of concluding the essay, we may mention a few more possibilities of crosscultural literary comparison and the cultural differentials the comparative approach will have to reckon with. The consideration of Shakespeare's last plays and of Kalidasa's plays together may have at a point to make reference to the theories and conventions of what one might call the European theories and traditions of tragicomedy such as those of Cinthio and Guarini and also to take into account Chapman's tragicomedies like *Monsieur D'Olive* and *The Gentleman Usher* with their mystique. The English religious poetry of the seventeenth century offers a good deal of scope for a study in correspondences with the Bhakti poetry of several Indian literatures, but the correspondences will have to be examined not without reference to the particular, denominational conventions, dogmas, practices and meditative paradigms of the poets on either side of the comparison. Possibly the concept of the avatar can serve as a lead-in into Milton's *Paradise Regained*, especially in understanding the poet's Christology in the poem. The application of the idea of the *avatar* to the poem may have to distinguish not only the levels of awareness and consciousness on the part of Christ of His manhood and Godhood but also similar modes of awareness or total lack of it on the part of an *avatar* like Rama as portrayed by Kamban and Valmiki respectively. Again, when exploring the lines of communication from Indian thought, myth and legend to the Romantic poets like Blake, Coleridge, Shelley and Southey, we will have to examine the media of transmission like Sir William Jones's poetry, especially his Hymns to Hindu deities as well as his prose and a novel set in India and about India and Indian thought like the Irish Lady Morgan's (also known as Sydney Owenson) *The Missionary* which was read avidly and absorbed by Shelley. But we will also have to keep in mind that Lady Morgan draws heavily on the writings including the poems of Jones in her image of India and Indian thought. Such means of mediation and channels of influence, it may appear, do not matter in themselves. But when it is a matter of communication of new cultures and new mythologies, the media of communication deeply condition the messages conveyed. The authenticity of the English poet's response to Indian ideas and myths depends on the authenticity of the image of India and things Indian received by him. As Eliot feared in *After Strange Gods* (p. 41), the mediation of Hindu and Buddhist thought to the West was through a 'romantic misunderstanding' of it. But the Western poets, including Eliot, had their sources of experience of Indian thought and myth through translations and understanding accounts of

Eastern thought and mythology. The nineteenth century French poet Leconte de Lisle wrote poems (such as "The Song of Ganga" and "The Vision of Brahma") based on French translations by Emile Burnouf (of the *Bhagavata*) and by Fauché of the *Ramayana* and the *Mahabharata*. In the case of this poet and his contemporary the Belgian Verharen's poem on Siva's burning of Manmata, the European Sanskritists's translations provided the source of their Indian poems.

Sruti/Smriti as Critical Analogues for Indo-English Literature

M. SIVARAMAKRISHNA

We can begin by citing a recent statement of the celebrated physicist David Bohm. Exploring the nature of meaning and the quest for it in contemporary culture, he says:

> Cultures are meaning, the East has one kind of meaning and the West another. It is the meaning of the West that makes it the West and the meaning of the East that makes it the East. I think that the difficult question related to these cultural meanings would have to be worked out in a *dialogue*. A dialogue between these cultures would bring us to something new.

The complexity of this dialogue is what we have to deal with. The intertexts of this dialogue are tradition and modernity and if this is to become a dialogue and not a sterile monologue of imposed aesthetic and rhetorical paradigms, we ought to have a 'second sight' of our own. This is an attempt at identifying the nature of that sight.

India has a vast, almost unique, philosophic, aesthetic and literary hinterland which cannot be brushed aside as an amorphous lump. This would be to surrender oneself to the tyranny of an insistent present which is in reality an unawareness of a past which impinges on and determines the present. Moreover, Indian philosophical texts—texts of perennial philosophy and pyschology—are receiving thoughtful attention and qualified acceptance in the scientific and intellectual milieu of the West. True, the dent is marginal but perceptible and where it is made, enduring. If a Krishnamurti impinges on the consciousness of a physicist of the stature of David Bohm and in turn makes him revise significantly his model of time and space – and more such sober examples, not sensational and goody goody ones, can be cited – then, it is imperative that we have a second look at our own aesthetic and critical insights. Above all, Sanskritists are vociferous in defending classical approaches to a literary text. The implicit national fervour is no excuse if this tall claim is not demonstrably proved by applying those approaches and categories to the texts available today even in English. If in the process these approaches are found anachronistic, the need is all the more for identifying the enduring residue from the anachronistic mass. In effect, there can be no better context than an Indo-English literary text to contemporize what are alleged to be the last words in philosophy, aesthetics and criticism.

II

We have to preface our further remarks by one basic tendency in explorations of tradition and modernity. With its insistence on individuality, modernity has led to what Ananda Coomaraswamy has called "a confusion of *originality* with *novelty*." Elaborating this confusion he adds that "it is of the essence of 'tradition' that something is kept alive; and as long as this is the case, it is as erroneous to speak of a 'mechanical' transmission from generation to generation as it is to suppose that the elements of culture can be mechanically borrowed from one people by another. It is only because our academic science acquaints us for the most part only with dead or dying traditions indeed, traditions that have been deliberately killed by the representatives of a supposedly higher culture, and because of our own individualistic insistence upon *novelty* that we are so little conscious of the absolute originality of even the most conservative" art.

Thus if mechanical transmission and borrowing are errors, the binary opposition of tradition and modernity on which most discussions hinge is equally indefensible. Whether they are opposed or whether they are transpositional is not of much concern. What is more relevant is to locate a complex in Indic philosophical thought which is a very close approximation – and a very subtle model – to these two. Such a model is embodied in the intersecting perceptions of what

Hindu philosophers identified as *sruti* and *smriti*. Whatever the theological debates about *sruti*, it has enough resilience to suggest that core of anything which endures. Literally "revelation," it is "that which has been perceived through hearing." Its meaning is never questioned but always established by debate. Representing "supreme and undebatable authority," it is inviolate. Thus *sruti*, if contemporized, would mean the enduring residue of a tradition. How complex a literary phenomenon *sruti* is, becomes, partly at least, clear if we look at the much misunderstood idea of *apaurusheya*. This is not an irrational denial of authorship or causal thinking. Nor does it mean that there was no mind behind it. When it affirms the truth as that which is heard, *sruti* is, in effect, suggesting, as Raimundo Panikar has pointed out, a mode "to purify our relationship with the text and to avoid idolatry" and tyranny of the author. According to this insight, "what has no author is the relation between the word and its meaning and object."

Once *sruti* is understood as, also, freedom from any authorial voice arbitrarily assigning personal meaning to the text, this crystallizes into tradition – the impersonal wisdom – which rescues us from the merely temporal/spatial intentions of any specific historical context. Therefore, that which is "heard" initially achieves fullness of responses by being "perceived, understood, realized." It is, in effect, "the sound – meaning aspect of reality" and *sruti* is that universality the value of which is rooted in the "actual existential act of really hearing" it.

This existential act involves the process of contemporizing. In other words, tradition, *sruti,* needs to be mediated through modes stemming from the contingency of contemporary situation. In effect, *sruti* is *anadi* and *ananta*, without beginning and without end. Yet it has to manifest, be discovered *in time*. Hence its counterpart *smriti*. Shorn of its pejorative associations, *smriti* constitutes the cluster of socio-political, economic and familial factors which redefine *sruti*. Therefore, *sruti* is eternal but within a temporal/spatial complex which is *smriti*. Both are intersecting points of a complex unified consciousness which functions harmoniously as a totality. In fact, even *smritis* are discoveries of eternal laws in nature. They do not promulgate law but discover the *dharma*.

To be more precise, what is *heard* (*sruti*) is localized in and through what is *remembered*. What is heard can become effective in and through what is *recalled*. The recall is memory and *memory* when it crystallizes becomes habit and habits, rationalized, ratified, become codes. On another level, *sruti* is the sacred, *smriti* the secular but both are kept in creative tension.

From the *Sruti/Smriti* paradigm – if taken approximately as tradition/contemporaneity model – we also get corresponding thematic motifs (at least indigenous thematic naming of motifs). Instead of the highly equivocal modernity/tradition, progress/backwardness, revolution/passivity binaries, usual in our literary frames, we can introduce *nihsreyasa* and *abhyudaya* as balancing motifs keeping aesthetic texts in creative tension. These are basic perspectives each defining and channeling the other. *Abhyudaya* (which is regulated by *smritis*) corresponds roughly to well-being on the secular level, the legitimate pursuit of goals which are biologically imperative, socially compulsive. These are the detectable, the relishable – what the *Katha Upanishad* names as *preyas* – crystallized in the two motives of *artha* and *kama*. *Artha* and *kama* are correspondences in the Indian context of the Marxist and the Freudian motifs.

But then these are not values absolutely validated, or abstractly condemned. They are extraordinarily powerful motives and determinants of character and action. But when they cease to be positive, they are then blown out of all proportion and, instead of being oriented to ends other than those implicit in themselves become self-destructive. There is then what David Schrum called "a disharmony between the particulars of living and the framework of its whole."

Nihsreyasa represents these firm orientations – the checks and balances – which subsume and channel *artha* and *kama*. Rather, this is not so much taming as a recycling of the tremendous energy inherent in the biological and the addictive to achieve the transcendent regulated by the holistic.

One can get the impression that all this is theological idiom. But, then the theological in Indic traditions is, almost at every step, capable of being transposed into the psychological. As such, these can be restated as a map of purposive concern reflecting a technology of self-regulation. Thus, this map of actualization rests on the basic "*envisioning* of one's true, intrinsic nature" which is *dharma*; "meaningfully giving expression to that nature is *artha; desiring* to actualize the unfoldment of one's truest nature is *kama* and ultimately transcending all relative modes of achievement is *moksha*." All of which suggest a frame of reference invaluable and indispensable for contemporary Indo-English texts, too.

This hinterland of value-systems is, obviously, highly relevant in identifying the thematic preoccupations of Indo-English literature. There is no question here of merely tradition/modernity conflict. It is a question of the holistic subsuming the parts. Thus Raja Rao would, from one perspective, portray a situation where these values are interiorized and salvaged but at the cost of what seems to be a disregard of the exterior. His fiction dramatizes a heroic attempt to rescue a value system. Both the attempt and the value system are authentic but authentic as *literature*, as literary *alamkaras* because of their incapacity to tackle the existential realities. In other words, even when *dharma* and *moksha* are deemed as definite determinants, the exigencies of a new historical reality make them suspect as pleasant palliatives to drown awareness of this reality. In an ethos where the minimum of *artha* and *kama* are lacking in objective correlatives of fulfilment, the dialectic of the serpent and the rope is bound to be suspect. But, if the holistic scheme is kept in view, Raja Rao's fiction is seen for what it is: basically a quest for the self denuded of its illusions. Once this perspective is kept in view, we will think twice before saying that Raja Rao's characters are metaphysical abstractions. They are bound to be that if we cling merely to the Western categories of narration.

Similarly, in Anand we find the quest for *artha* and *kama* given a tremendous thrust, an exclusive preoccupation, which colours his entire perspective on history and myth. His is an indictment of a society which is the cruel end-product of a total distortion of the value-systems outlined above. Historical reasons explain this distortion but this distortion itself should never lead us to the fatal mistake of rejecting the values.

Basing himself on the realistic mode, Anand approximates most closely to the Western novel. And reminiscent of other social historians, his novels offer a trenchant, often very valid, criticism of the decadent aspects of Indian ethos. About the authenticity of Anand's creative ferment, there can be little doubt. This is the reason why humanists find him very "charming," e.g. Forster.

But if the value-system outlined above is kept in view, there is a whole new approach sustained by Anand's fiction. He envisaged a society where legitimate channelling of the energies for the fulfilment of *artha* and *kama* is effortlessly guaranteed through viable social structures. But the problem is, without restraint and awareness of limits to fulfilment, *artha* and *kama* are fatal energies which, in an open, emerging affluent society impel a person to corner all the resources towards their fulfilment for himself. Bakhas even now do not have any chance in Indian society. Not cornering but confering becomes possible through a voluntary restraint – in short, through deliberate renunciation, a voluntary impulse which leads us to assert freedom from dependence and slavery on resources for fulfilment on *artha* and *kama* as absolute and not relative energies.

Anand's version of an egalitarian society is, thus, without correctives, a charmingly romantic, if not a totally misleading one. For between the alternate model of a self in a socialist society – denuded of ultimate values – and the model of a self lapping up things and experiences to compensate for having starved so long there is hardly anything worthwhile to choose.

To put the above discussion in perspective: Raja Rao's accent is on *nihsreyas*, the electable: Anand's forte is *abhyudaya*, the delectable. Each has its own viability *within* the framework given, but *together* they make for the synthetic view. If both these are not properly balanced, the resulting predicament is the preoccupation of the English novelists of the 60s to date. The fiction of Anita Desai, Nayantara Sahgal and Arun Joshi – and on a lower key that of Bharati Mukherjee and other women novelists – is shot through with the inevitable alienation and despair of an affluent section of society. Most of these affluent protagonists find alienation a comforting dogma to order their experience. Two questions can therefore be raised about their fiction: is alienation the result of affluence, the affluent model of society? If this is conceded, what affirmative value does this fiction possess in an ethos where the majority of people dream of this affluence as their cherished goal? i.e., are scarcity and plenitude – and the implicit definitions of progress and development – exclusively economic in content and context? (The above scheme answers these questions – if one can work them out).

III

Narayan is not mentioned above alongside Anand and Raja Rao. The reason for this is simple; his fiction reflects basically the Indian belief in character and its nature – *Swabhava* – as determined by *gunas* (energies, qualities etc.). Hence this section examines the criterion of *guna*.

Gunas are in Indian ethos closely linked to the basic syndrome of *samskaras*. These are antecedent predisposition which impel one towards a particular course of action. *Samskaras* give rise to predominant passions, *gunas*, which are decisive determinants of action. If they go "wrong" even *that* is entirely appropriate. If they lead us to the "right" it is equally acceptable. Once the logic of *gunas* is accepted, character is determined. Whatever changes occur they are intimations of a surfacial reality and the essential *samskara* remains unchanged. Allied to this *samskara* is the faith in the balancing forces implicit in nature, however flawed it apparently is. Belief in the assertion of the underlying moral order remains unaffected. Therefore, even tentative discords only succeed in "reassembling the forces of stability." Thus, as Herbert Fingarette puts it, "Karmic law is not the edict of the All-Powerful Disciplinarian, not an expression of will accompanied by the threat of sanctions. It purports to be factual description: somehow or other, things do eventually 'balance out' in the moral realm."

These *gunas* – *sattva*, *rajas* and *tamas* – whatever their constituent impulses and dynamis are what Coomaraswamy called "characteristic willing." They impel a person towards an 'action' and the correspondingly relentless 'reaction'. Since these are basic energies of one's being to brand them as negative or positive is pointless. Moreover, these energies are fluid and transpositional and while involving movement also imply transcendence. Since there is movement, there is also apparent evolution.

> The three types sattva, rajas, and tamas are . . . the material cause of the psychic and the physical universe, and their characteristics are known from their products. Each of them stands for a distinct aspect of reality in the physical realm and a distinct characteristic of psychic experiences in the realm of thought and feeling.

> Though the three gunas form the material of the universe, both physical and psychic, and though they coexist and cohere, one of them upon any specific occasion predominates over the others.

What is significant here is that *gunas* are both psychic dispositions and aspects of physical reality. If on the psychic level they colour thoughts and feeling, on the physical level they are extensions of the same: embodied and enshrined concretions of the psychic. Hence arises a peculiar intersection of the "physical" and the "psychic" which, together, constitutes a crucial critical nexus. To illustrate, if the temple in Narayan's *The Guide* is a physical locale representing the self poised in the ambience of tranquillity – *sattva* – this becomes a logical extension of the evolution of Raju from a state of *tamas* and *rajas* to incipient *sattva*. Even earlier, one notices that the seduction by Raju of Rosie – an apparent descent into the *tamasic* – is counterpointed by the locale of the hotel – an apotheosis of the rootless and the homeless, – coming together for convenience and not a uniting in terms of shared myths and sacraments.

Here we find *guna* offering us dependable tools of analysis in regard to character vis-a-vis setting and background (an analysis which is equally relevant to writers as apparently divergent as Anand and Chaman Nahal on the one side and Anita Desai and Nayantara Sahgal on the other) but *gunas* also offer, as Edwin Gerow has suggested, a distinct Indian configuration of plot.

Before we go to this aspect, one inference from the Indian concept of *gunas* – as essential tag of character traits – needs to be made. This is the most important 'fact' that the entire gamut of actions impelled by the *gunas* takes place in the world projected by the mind, in the world the dialectic of which is described by Indian darshanas as *maya*. *Maya* is both real and unreal and, as such, for the mind-born enquiry committed to neat logic, marked by pervasive contradiction. If it is regarded as unreal, the unreality lies in our attempt to grasp it – the world of *maya* – through concepts and forms, by thought and name. If it is regarded as real, then we are prone to commit the error rooted in the corresponding unawareness: the error is, in effect, "not the appearance as such but the forgetfulness that the appearance is appearance."

But appearance also *is*. It is *vyavaharika satya*, the "reality" by which we live and love, "catch our trains and catch our colds." Its analogue is a holographic image: it has length, breadth and width but it is a projection one can't touch. It is real for all *practical* purposes but the reactions and responses it sets in motion are real to the extent a mimetic rendering is *real*. Therefore within this flawed reality – rent by fragmentation – we have the wholeness of art and literature. But this wholeness and other qualities are apparently so. For, what takes place is what *seems* to take place.

The development of plot from this point of view is psychological like Indian philosophy itself – rather than formal, as in western critical ethos. Therefore, changes in plot and development of character take place in the world of appearance. Since *gunas* colour consciousness – itself colourless – any development of character and incident can only lead to and result in the assertion of the original state of stability, the disturbing of which brought about the play of the *gunas* with all that it entails. The upshot is what a character in Anita Desai articulates: "Purely detached acceptance of a world not worth realizing." Not worth realizing because realizing it is to make it *real* and that the world of *maya* is not.

Therefore, narrational development does take place but without altering the essential psyche. In effect, *gunas* make it appear as if development is possible but development is, in the Indian classical view, a temporary irruption – if it is good i.e., *sattvic*, it reinforces the original psychic stability, if it is *rajasic* or *tamasic* it impels the forces of stability to assert themselves by reassembling the forces of order. As Edwin Gerow has put it:

> The dramatic eventuation . . . is not the plot, seen as a play of forces and suggesting or clarifying previously inexplicit or unrealized relationships, not the development of the story to a 'conclusion', but is rather what one might call an 'anti-plot': the reintegration of an original state – dynamic to be sure but stable – which has for a time been threatened with dislocation. All that 'happens' is that the miasma of confusion created by the demonic 'irruption' is finally dissipated. All that can happen is what we began with: the stable cosmos.

What Gerow says is, of course, specially relevant to Narayan. But even when the novelist appears to be radical and intensely contemporary, this view of character and plot – that 'evil', disorder etc., is "a mistake of the intellect rather than the result of the flaw of character" – is a far more rewarding approach than the extant ones stemming from realistic/symbolic frames. For instance, characters in Anita Desai seem gradually – as do her plots – to veer to this view of finding the Indian situation as amenable to the dialectic of *maya* (in fact, one of her characters is named after this most complex of Indian insights). They thus move away from a monolithic view to an accommodative one where even the exasperating contradictions become integral components of the whole. In terms of structure, the alienation based on what initially is regarded as irrevocable disorder is seen progressively as a stage, a part of a cycle of growth, decay and regeneration: from the island we return to the mainland. Once the Hindu view of order and disorder are introduced as criteria, we get a more relevant perspective of evaluation. The 'growth' of the character is obviously seen not as *realization* of a deeper, holistic truth which always *is*.

Obviously, the most sustained and pervasive effort is needed to make this view of character (an offshoot of *gunas* and *samskaras*) and plot and development of action (within the paradigms of *maya* and order/disorder) illumine Indo-English creative writing, especially fiction.

An important aspect, again, in this regard is the Hindu nomenclature regarding narratives which is itself a significant pointer to the fact that narratives were considered as tentative formal differentiations within the larger undifferentiated continuum of consciousness which is the Ground of all Forms. This is the reason why stories were conceived as waves in the vast ocean of narrative: *Katha Sagara*. We have therefore spirals of stories with different narrators becoming voices reflecting on different aspects of the story. Thus arises an extraordinarily sophisticated cluster of "frames" rising and dissolving endlessly. In this sense, plot is vision "embodied."

Hence the suggestive formal chapterization named *Ucchwas* and *taranga*. The latter is literally "breathing out," a formal pause in narrative, equivalent perhaps to our 'sections' in chapters. Suggesting both a formal stop which is 'real' but real within the larger integral, undifferentiated formlessness – the basis of all forms. Analogously, *taranga* is a relatively more 'weighty' wave, perhaps a chapter. Since water is the most conformable and fluid of images, all narratives are inexhaustible causations and forms.

Once these narrational forms are kept in view, one can reinforce, deepen and intensify our criteria of time in English fiction (and other genres) with the related motifs of beginnings and endings, and above all of myths. For instance, one can temper our awareness of Narayan's beginnings and endings – notwithstanding Frank Kermodes and Edward Saids – in terms of not merely "open" endings but also in the frames of mythic plots and their implicit dialectical interplay which, like the Greek view, is "a natural process in which everything recurred in periodical cycles, so that nothing really new ever happened." Character in this sense is poised equably between the 'ephemeral' and the 'eternal'. As Zimmer puts it: "We are taught to recognize the divine, the impersonal sphere of eternity, revolving ever and agelessly through time. But we are also taught to esteem the transient sphere of the duties and pleasures of individual existence, which is as real and as vital to the living man, as a dream to the sleeping soul."

IV

If the introduction of the word "divine" appears naive – if not offensive – then we can take another less controversial word: myth. This aspect is, potentially, the most fruitful, but the least examined, in the Indo-English context. In fact, not many critics of this literature seem at all to be aware of the fact that these myths and their symbolic meanings are "the pictorial script of India's ultimately changeless wisdom." As such they are indispensable sources for identifying and evaluating the recurrent concerns of the English creative writer.

Myth in this context is basically *purana* and involves several perspectives – on time, death and fate – and the patterning of narratives. Blending of fable and fact, history and legend, with apparent digressions which are didactic and metaphysical, with characters who range from deities, demons to gods and humans, alongside cosmological theories and oral traditions – the *purana* is, in effect, an encyclopedia of culture and religion. As such, it is bound to be an inexhaustible source for the creative writer. But, for literary criticism, the perspectives should transcend the consideration of myth as merely a *source*. Myth is a centre of consciousness – a continuum of time/timelessness paradox involving and balancing the several polarities of our existence: the secular and the sacred, good and evil, the prelogical, and logical etc. In effect, myth is – as in Narayan, Raja Rao and Anita Desai – an assertion of the sacred through the profane.

Thus myth is both a technique suggesting structural parallels and a vision of life based on affirmation. Therefore, to evaluate a text in terms of mythic technique while withholding consent from the vision of life reflected in myth is to be guilty of the modern heresy of secularization. This heresy has plagued the criticism of even such a pervasively mythic writer as Narayan. In this sense, myth is artistic form given to sacred images of life which persist in literature either consciously or unconsciously. And the mythic structure could also involve the skilful use of one of its indispensable components: dream and its kin, fantasy. As the *Mandukya Upanishad* argues, the states of waking, dream and deep sleep are poised against the backdrop of an unchanging, undifferentiated consciousness. Therefore, transformations of the self in narratives are only discoveries of its original state of being. In other words, narratives as reflections of the undifferentiated state of being caught in the web *maya* can only be regarded in terms of and as *alamkaras*.

V

All narrative structures are oriented to the evoking of emotion as a preliminary process to the ultimate realization of a "state" denuded of emotion. As Ananda Coomaraswamy puts it:

> The original intention of intelligible form was not to entertain us, but literally to 're-mind' us. The chant is not for the approval of the ear, nor the picture for that of the eye (although these senses can be taught to approve the splendour of truth, and can be trusted when they have been trained), but to effect such a transformation of our being as is the purpose of all ritual acts. It is, in fact, the radial arts that are the most 'artistic' because the most 'correct' as they must be if they are to be effectual.

This brings us to the discussion of *alamkaras* both linguistic and emotive. In fact Sanskrit poetics has an abundance of critical concepts which in its overall complexity puts even the most sophisticated modern ideas in this regard to shade. We have the criteria of *vakrokti, vaichitri, auchitya, chamatkar, riti, guna* etc. Above all, there are the classical perceptions of *dhvani* and *rasa*, the most complex in the entire range of Indian aesthetics.

Dhvani gives us extremely useful tools of analysis ranging from linguistic nuances to discrepancies stemming from different situations and character patterns. It is, in effect, one of the most important bases of irony—an irony ranging from the comically resolved one (as in Narayan) to the basic absurdity as in Anita Desai which can be neither resolved nor dissolved but is to be absored into the implicate order of the wholeness. Above all, *dhvani* as suggestion gives us a vast range of ambiguity both situational and linguistic.

An extension of *dhvani* is *rasa*, the classic Indian paradigm of the function and value of emotion in literature. It is basically an offshoot, in sensibility, of the activating of intrinsic feelings so that the imbedded emotions are evoked through stylized characters and situations which become basic determinants. In other words, *rasa* generalizes emotions through objective correlatives and therefore implies a transcendence which is emblematic of the final release from the *laukika* into the *paralaukika*. As René Daumal has pointed out, *Rasa* (translated by him as *taste* "is the moment of conscience (and consciousness) that a true work of art should evoke in whoever has an interior being and a measure for judging; a moment of waking to oneself arising from a particular emotion provoked by a true work of art."

"Waking to oneself" is epiphany: shock of recognition, relevant for all literary forms, and not necessarily to poetic ones. Therefore, *rasa* can be applied to Indo-English narratives as a comprehensive structure of evaluation.

Viewed thus, *sruti/smriti* is a vast complex of metaphysical, psychological and aesthetic analogue which offers a pervasive critical model of great potential. To claim and appropriate this potential by actualizing it is a function which awaits Indo-English critical intelligence.

Images of Guru in the Indian Novel: A Comparative Study

A. RAMAKRISHNA RAO

India is known for its philosophical achievement, especially for its monistic view of the self. It is a land of saints, sages, seers, sadhus, and sanyasis, who have shown to the common man the path of realization. As C.S. Lewis rightly says, "All over the world, until quite modern times, the direct insight of the mystics and the reasonings of the philosophers percolated to the mass of people by authority and tradition; they could be received by those who were no great reasoners themselves in the concrete form of myth and ritual and the whole pattern of life. In the conditions produced by a century or so of Naturalism, plain men are being forced to bear the burdens which plain men were never expected to bear before."[1] When a plain man tries to play the role of a guru, an awkward situation ensues, sometimes leading to absurd and fantastic faking or sometimes, an ironic crisis potentially tragic. For example, Sasthi Brata's *The Sensuous Guru: The Making of Mystic President*[2] dramatizes the progress of Chakravarti from the role of a guru who initiates disciples in the practice of *hathayoga* to that of a seducer and exploiter of innocence, and ultimately to that of the first Hindu president of the United States of America. R.K. Narayan's *The Guide* is a revealing and interesting creative comment on the efforts of a lay man to get out of an awkward hole which destiny thrusts on him. In Ruth Prawer Jhabvala's *The New Dominion*, we come across Swamiji, who has an *ashram* situated ten miles away from Benares. Lee, a young American tourist, who goes to the *ashram* in search of peace, describes the scene as follows:

> The room was dominated by a large coloured picture of Swamiji's own guru, a very holy man who wore no clothes and sat on a deer skin. Underneath this there was a big velvet armchair with an antimacassar embroidered by one of the disciples and here Swamiji sat with two devotees waving a peacock fan over him. They all faced the picture of the holy guru and Swamiji sitting beneath it, and then how they sang! With what inspiration! Of course it was he who inspired them. It was he who sang out the names of God and invited them to call after him – 'Rama!' he sang 'Gopala! Hari! Krishna!' in his melodious, smiling voice and then who could resist following him and also calling out those sweet names and being filled with the savour of them. But however loudly, however devoutly they sang, it was never enough for Swamiji – always he begged for more, always he led them higher and higher, to sing out louder and louder – 'Rama! Gopala! Hari! Krishna!' – he incited them to break out again and again into those names, to fetch them forth out of hearts that must be coaxed to overflow with the love of them.[3]

As it often happens in Jhabvala's novels, even in the text under review, we notice the play of irony. Starting as the description of Swamiji's daily routine, it ends with Swamiji *inciting* his disciples to chant the divine names. As we follow the career of Swamiji, we notice that he is more interested in expanding his activities abroad and for this purpose he woos the foreign tourists who come to the *ashram*. Moreover, Swamiji is not free from those drives and impulses which vitiate reason and make one an animal. Jhabvala's irony is such that it is not easy to determine whether Swamiji has genuine spiritual power or he is just a fake.

In this rapidly changing Indian socio-cultural milieu, the position of a Swamiji or a sanyasi in society is quite embarrassing, if not totally suspect. In Kamala Markandaya's *A Silence of Desire*, we have a swami, or sanyasi, who brings about a minor upheaval in Dandekar's family. Dandekar's wife, Sarojini, becomes the disciple of the Swami, because of her conviction that he might show her a way to get rid of a growth in her womb. She is not the only disciple of the swami. Many women and men with all sorts of physical and psychic ailments frequent the place where the swami stays. Dandekar develops an unwarranted suspicion regarding his wife's absence at home. Obsessed with ill feeling, he teases his wife. When an enquiry into the swami's activities takes place, nobody is in a position to state the facts as they are regarding the swami's bona fides. But one point seems to be certain: the swami imparts a sort of conviction and spiritual sustenance to a number of patients who fail to get admission in hospital as inpatients. This suggests that whatever may be the spiritual attainment of the swami, he does service to the suffering humanity.

II

Philosophically speaking, a guru or a swami is a realized soul. No wonder that even in modern India, we have gurus and *gurukulams*. Ramaswamy in *The Serpent and the Rope* proposes to himself that the only way left for him to get out of the problematic of the serpent and the rope is to seek the feet of his guru in Trivandrum. Like Aldous Huxley's protagonists in *Eyeless in Gaza* and *Time Must Have a Stop* who graduate themselves from sensuality to self-knowledge through the mediation of an exponent of the Perennial Philosophy, Ramaswamy's spiritual quest terminates, or is supposed to terminate, at the feet of a guru. Huxley's exponents of the Perennial Philosophy, Dr. James Miller in *Eyeless in Gaza* and Bruno Rontini in *Time Must Have a Stop* incessantly talk about non-violence, non-attachment, and a unitive knowledge of the divine ground. Nowhere in the text do we come across any clue that demonstrates the validity of their philosophical ideas. Although we cannot make this kind of comment on Maugham's *The Razor's Edge*, we encounter an identical problem in assessing the spiritual quest of Maugham's protagonist, who visits India.

Hermann Hesse's *Siddhartha* seems to place the entire problematic we have been discussing in its proper perspective. Hesse's title should not make us think that it defends Buddhist philosophy. Strictly speaking, it is a very subtle comment on Buddhism. After hearing the Buddha's teachings, Siddhartha tells him, "I have learned nothing through teachings, and so I think, O Illustrious One, that nobody finds salvation through teachings. To nobody, O Illustrious

One, can you communicate in words and teachings what happened to you in the hour of your enlightenment. The teachings of the enlightened Buddha embrace much, they teach much – how to live righteously, how to avoid evil. But there is one thing that this clear, worthy instruction does not contain; it does not contain the secret of what the Illustrious One himself experienced – he alone among hundreds of thousands. That is what I thought and realized when I heard your teachings. That is why I am going on my way – not to seek another and better doctrine, for I know there is none, but to leave all doctrines and all teachers and to reach my goal alone – or die."[4] A character comparable to Siddhartha in Indian fiction is Sribilas in Tagore's *Chaturanga*. In the quadrilateral tension and the emotional conflict that the novel dramatizes, the guru, Lilanandaswami, is a silent spectator of the love-triangle that gradually emerges, involving Sachis, Sribilas, and Damini. Sribilas watches with agony the attraction-and-repulsion-complex that grows between Sachis and Damini. Sachis repeatedly tells him that woman is a symbol of *prakriti* and intercourse with *prakriti* would imprison one's consciousness. In a crucial phase of their relationship, Sribilas tells Sachis, "I grant you all this . . . but let me tell you, my dear, that I did not lay this all-pervading snare with my own hands, nor do I know to evade it altogether. And since it is beyond us to ignore it, I should say the true way of spiritual discipline would be to acknowledge nature and yet rise above it. That is not the way we are going, whatever you may say. And so we end up wriggling and floundering, trying to clip and prune truth to halves."[5] "Trying to clip and prune truth to halves" is precisely Siddhartha's complaint against his father, the Samanas, the Buddha, and Kamaswami. Siddhartha tells his friend Govinda, "I am telling you what I have discovered. Knowledge can be communicated. One can find it, live it, be fortified by it, do wonders through it, but one cannot communicate and teach it. . . . When the Illustrious Buddha taught about the world, he had to divide it into Samsara and Nirvana, into illusion and truth, into suffering and salvation. One cannot do otherwise. There is no other method for those who teach. But this world itself, being in and around us, is never one-sided. Never is a man or a deed wholly Samsara or wholly Nirvana; never is a man wholly a saint or a sinner. This only seems so because we suffer the illusion that time is something real. Time is not real, Govinda. I have realized this repeatedly. And if time is not real, then the dividing line that seems to lie between this world and eternity, between suffering and bliss, between good and evil, is also an illusion."[6]

III

Tagore and Hesse seem to suggest that what a guru can achieve at best is to place one in direct focus with one's self. Faulkner's Sam Fathers in *The Bear* and R.K. Narayan's Master in *A Tiger for Malgudi* are fine specimens of the image we have been explicating in the foregoing analysis. Issac McCaslin learns humility, patience, skill and reverence from Sam Fathers in such a way that "It seemed to him that at the age of ten he was witnessing his own birth."[7] His decision to dissociate himself from his patrimony stems from the knowledge of the self he acquires through the mediation of Sam Fathers. The knowledge of the self consists in realizing that "there is a wisdom beyond even that learned through suffering necessary for a man to distinguish between liberty and licence."[8] It is precisely this kind of wisdom that the tiger learns from its master in *A Tiger for Malgudi*. Narayan, the reluctant guru, without violating the canons of realism, creates a swamiji who helps a tiger achieve direct focus with his self. The narrative voice, inhering in the tiger, tells us, "I would not blame you for keeping your distance – I myself shuddered at my own reflection on the still surface of the pond while crouching for a drink of water, not when I was really a wild beast but after I came under the influence of my Master and learnt to question, 'Who am I?'"[9] The preceding citation amply demonstrates what a guru can do to a disciple. Speaking from the Hindu philosophical perspective, a guru's grace should be such that it generates a philosophical and spiritual dialogue which may reach its culmination "Thou art that" as an answer to the question "Who am I?"

NOTES

1. C.S. Lewis, "Answers to Misgivings," in *Miracles: A Preliminary Study* (1947; rpt. Glassgow: Collins, 1974), p. 46.
2. Sasthi Brata, *The Sensuous Guru: The Making of a Mystic President* (New Delhi: Sterling, 1980).

3. R. Prawer Jhabvala, *A New Dominion* (London: John Murray, 1972), p. 66.
4. Hermann Hesse, *Siddhartha*, trans. Hilda Rosner (New York: New Directions), pp. 27-28.
5. Rabindranath Tagore, *Chaturanga*, trans. Asok Mitra (New Delhi: Sahitya Akademi), p. 62.
6. *Siddhartha*, p. 115.
7. William Faulkner, *The Bear, Go Down, Moses and Other Stories* (1942; rpt. Harmondsworth: Penguin, 1960), p. 148.
8. *Ibid*., p. 221.
9. R.K. Narayan, *A Tiger for Malgudi* (Mysore: IndianThought Publications, 1983), p. 12.

Context-Bound Sloka-Dialogue

S. LAXMANA MURTHY

The origin and function of the narrative have long been subjects of study. Its mythic relation allied to song, dance and ritual impulse lies buried deeply in every narrative whatever its form. Just as epic, ballad and the variety of heroic poetry have to make provision for the absence of dance and song by verbal devices, short story and novel and the variety of prose fiction have to find room for the mythic resonance. Hence the archetypal patterns linking a modern narrative to a remote Greek myth. In fact nothing can be closer to human psyche than myth reflected in themes, images and narrative patterns. Every narrative mode is intended to communicate the message with verbal devices, suggest a great deal through symbols, and finally light up a darkling corner in the consciousness as Ritual does. Narrative structure stems from a situation and strives to bring in the atmosphere proper to it. Antiphonal and stichomythic terms hint at the basic need and function of the narrative. Repeated efforts at it converge on a set of patterns relevant to the historical and cultural context, allowing free play for creative imagination, since the context not only facilitates easy communication, but also acts as a spring-board. Once the context is familiar, assent is given, and one would not demur the length of the narrative, and its otherwise unwelcome features like anachronistic inconsistencies. An attempt is made here to examine the context-bound sloka dialogue against this background.

II

There are various modes of adapting the sloka-dialogue. It may be, for instance, in the encyclopaedic epic like the *Mahabharata* or a catechism like *Prasna-Uttara-Ratna-Malika* or in a familiar devotional lyric like *Krishna-Karna-Amritam* or in a bunch of context-bound stories gathered in *Bhoja Charitram*.

III

There are two famous episodes in the *Mahabharata*, one of Savitri and the other relating to Yudhisthira's encounter with Yaksha. In the former, the impressive eloquence of Savitri outwits Yama and wins back the life of Satyavan. The narrative throughout illustrates the principles of Dharma while praising Yama. Savitri deftly seizes the opportunity and prays for progeny for the fourth boon.

Yamah: Vināsya Jivitam varam Chaturtham.
Varayasva Bhamini[1]

Savitri: Mamātmajam Satyavatasthathaurasam
Bharedubhābhyāmiha yatkulodvaham
Satam sutānām balavirya salinam
Idam Chaturtham varayami te varam.[2]

Yamah: Satam sutānām balaviryasālinām
Bhavishyati pritikaram tavābale
Parisramaste na bhavennripātmaje
Nivarta dūram hi pathastvamāgatā.[3]

---

1. Savitri, I will grant you the fourth boon. You ask for whatever you want except the life of Satyavan.
2. The fourth one may please be this:
   I want a hundred sons born of Satyavan and me. They should be strong, and win credit to the family.
3. Savitri, you will get a hundred sons who delight you. You are tired. You have already travelled very far. Please return home.

Savitri: Varātisargah sataputratā mama
Tvayaiva datto hriyate cha me patih
Varam vrine Jivatu satyavanayam
Tavaiva satyam vachanam bhavisyati.[4]

Yamah: Esa bhadre maya mukto bharta
te kulanandini.[5]

The dialogue merits a close study. The quiet beginning, the eloquent persuasion and the final triumph of Savitri show rare dexterity in composition. The sudden turn at the end to the discomfiture of Yama is brought about quite effortlessly as it were.

In the second episode Yudhisthira patiently answers the shrewd questions of Yaksha. The sloka-dialogue is different from that of the earlier episode. The question and the answer have the same form, the answer following the question quickly with the force characteristic of a repartee.

Yaksah: Kassatrurdurjayah pumsām kaseha vyādhiranantakah
Kidrisascha smritah sādhuh asādhuh kidrisasmritah.[6]

Yudhisthirah: Krodhastu durjayah satruh lobho
vyadhiranantakah
Sarvabhutahitah sādhuh asādhuh nirdayah smritah.[7]

---

4. You have granted me the boon of a hundred sons. You are taking away my husband. I want Satyavan brought back to life. That alone will make your words truthful.
5. Your husband is set free. You are fortunate indeed. You bring cheer to your family.
6. Who is the most invincible enemy of man?
Which is the incurable disease?
Who is good? Who is bad?
7. Anger is man's most invincible enemy
Avarice is the incurable disease
The one who loves all is good
Loveless one is bad.

The dialogue employs the epic convention of repeating the set phrases like "sapatnam jiva micchasi, Nakulam jiva micchasi, Nakulo yaksa jivatu." The sloka sequence is carefully structured to the end befitting the quiet dignity of Yudhisthira.

Prasna-Uttara-Ratna-Malika is a series of sixty five slokas attributed to Sankara. It is a composition of pithy lines in the form of a question-answer sequence. A single sloka may have in it two or more questions quickly followed by answers:

Bhagavan kimupādeyam
Guruvachanam heyamapicha kim akaryam
Ko guruh adhigata tattvah
Sisyahitaya udyatah satatam.[8]

Ko narakah paravasatā
Kim soukhyam sarvasanga viratiryā
Kim satyam bhutahitam
Priyam cha kim prāninām asavah.[9]

These two tiny slokas reveal the pattern. While in the *Mahabharata* the question-answer sequence is brought out in two separate slokas, here we find question and answer embedded in the same sloka with extreme

---

8. Sir, what is most welcome?
Guru's word.
What is hateful?
Evil.
Who is a teacher?
One who knows the truth and is always ready to help his pupil.
9. What is hell?
Slavery.
What is happiness?
Detachment.
What is truth?
The good of the living beings.
What is dear?
Life.

precision and directness. In any case, the device is employed in the huge compendium like the *Mahabharata* and the brief *Malika*. We may further notice that the question-answer sequence dramatizes the *Mahabharata* story, but in the *Malika* it is a plain series of independent questions and answers.

IV

What is plain and somewhat dry in the *Malika* is rendered interesting when the device is employed in *stotras* like *Krishna-Karna-Amritam*. The following sloka-dialogue is a dramatization of the context – the pranks of playful Krishna:

> Kastvam bāla balaniyah kimihate manmandirasankaya
> yuktam tannavanitapatravivare hastam kimartham nyaseh
> Matah kanchana vatsakam mrigayitum mā gā visādam ksanāt
> Ityevam varavallavi prativachana parah patu vaschakrapānih.[10]

Krishna's innocence is revealed within three lines with a worried milkmaid puzzled and pleased while Krishna replies confidently.

We may cite another sloka-dialogue from the same work. Here a youthful gopika discomfits Krishna, now a young man of course.

> Angulyā kah kavātam mahaprati kutile madhavah kim vasantsah
> No chakri kim kulalo nahi dharanidharah kim dvijihvah
> phanindrah

---

10. Dear me,
Who are you?
Bala's younger brother.
Why did you come here?
I mistook it my house.
Why did you then put your hand there in the butter pot?
Mother, just don't worry! I have been looking for a white calf that has strayed, maybe, it is there.
May this engaging Krishna protect us.

Nāham ghorāhimardi kimapi khagapatih no harih kim kapindrah
Ityevam gopakanya prativachanajitah patu vah chakrapanih.[11]

The dialogue is based on the *double-entendre* that is natural to Sanskrit. The smart girl keeps the boy at bay.

V

There are quite a few delightful stories in *Bhoja Charitram*. Many famous poets like Kalidasa and Bhavabhuti and also scholars like Mallinatha who are separated from one another by centuries are brought together, and there is an encounter for each of them with Bhoja, the great scholar king of 11th century. The anachronism does not trouble us as the stories present a lovely sport of poetry with clever conceits. This is not limited to poets and scholars alone. Ordinary men and women regale Bhoja with charming slokas. We will examine only those slokas which present a dialogue within.

There is an anecdote of Kalidasa meeting a young woman who parried off successfully many poets by reciting the first half of a sloka, while they failed to compose the second half as the convention required. She recites:

Kusume kusumotpattih sruyate na cha drisyate

Kalidasa completes it with

---

11. Who is there knocking the door?
Dear me, I am Madhava (Laxmi's husband).
You mean to say that spring has come.
No. I am Chakrin (Disc-bearer).
So a potter has come.
No. I am Dharanidhara (one who lifted the earth).
So you must be a double-tongued cobra.
No, dear, I am the one who killed a cobra.
Then you are a hawk.
No. I am Hari (Lord Vishnu).
What! A monkey!
May this outwitted Krishna protect us.

Bāle tava mukhāmbhoje dristam indivaradvayam.[12]

When on a hunting expedition Bhoja meets a tribal woman, and there ensues this dialogue:

Kā tvam putri narendra lubdhaka vadhūh haste kimetat palam
Ksāmam kim sehajam braveemi nripate yadyādarat sruyate
Gayanti tvadaripriyasrutatini tireshu siddhānganāh
Gitam gānatrinam charanti harināstenamisam durlabham.[13]

All these encounters depend heavily on poetic licenses. What matters is the skill with which a context is created for the dialogue.

There is yet another story of a tired traveller meeting Bhoja who enquired whence he came:

Kailasādaha māgatosmi kusali kim tatra mrityunjayah
Durvāravyasanāpanodita manāh panchatvamāpeswarah
Kim tasyāpi maheswarasya vasatih sokādivhirdūyate
No chet sarvagunāsrayah pibati kim hālāhalam dārunam.[14]

---

12. We have heard it said that a flower comes out of a flower. We have not seen it though.
My dear, I find looking at you, two blue lotuses on the white one.
13. Who are you?
King, I am a tribal woman.
What is that you hold in your hand?
A piece of meat.
Why is there so little of it?
I will tell you, if you choose to hear.
The women of your enemies whom you have killed in war have wept bitterly and caused a river of tears to flow. Sitting on the river bank, the heavenly nymphs sing so sweetly that the deer forget to graze. Hence the scarcity of meat.
14. Where are you from?
I have come from Kailasa.
Is the one who defeated death (Siva) safe?
Lord Siva, of course, died of great mental agony.
What do you mean? Even Siva's household in trouble?
Otherwise why would Siva take poison?

There was this agonizing domestic disharmony which forced Siva to end his life by taking poison:

> Hartum vānchati vāhanam ganapatah bhaūshā bhujauyah sadā
> Tam vāhascha sadāmanasya taruni vahopi nagānanam
> Gouri jahnusutāmasūyati katānātham lalātanalah
> Nirvinnah sa popow kutumba kalahat Isopi halahalam.[15]

Siva's assets disappeared soon after:

> Gangā sāgaramambaram sasikalā nagādhipo bhūtalam
> Vahniryajnatalam vivesa vrishabho dhūrvāhakah karshakam
> Artham dānavavairina girijayāpyardham sivasyahritam
> Sarvajnatvam adhiswaratvam agamat tvām mām che bhiksātanam.[16]

The Siva-myth is exploited fully, and it is given an engaging secular interpretation.

The contextual sloka-dialogue has many interesting forms. The story form merits study in the light of the fact that sloka-dialogue shapes it to a great extent and enlivens it by dramatizing.

---

15. The Cobra round his neck wants to eat up Ganapathi's rat. Kumara's peacock wants to kill the Cobra. Parvathi's lion attacks the elephant-headed Ganapathi. The moon on Siva's head is scorched by the fire on his forehead. His two wives – Parvathi and Ganga – are never at peace. Helpless and upset by the family quarrels; even Siva took poison.
16. Ganga flowed into the ocean.
The moon went up the sky.
The cobras slipped into the outhills,
The fire on his head reached the sacrificial altar.
The bull went to plough the fields.
Vishnu got his money, Parvathi took the other half.
Wisdom and power came to you
I have, of course, got his begging bowl. (Hence I am here.)

'Writer's Block' and the Indian Poet's 'English Chains'

C. SUBBA RAO

I

From time to time we hear of the Muse being "unchained" in Indian poetry in English. Despite the general decline in the use of English in the country, the paradox of a sudden flowering of Indian Poetry in English recently cannot but be greeted with surprise and optimism. We have also been surprised by a new wave in fiction towards the end of the eighties. Everyone knows that one swallow does not make a summer although one is grateful for that one at least.

The Indian poet in English has for long been regarded with a mixture of condescension and contempt. He is forced to feel apologetic about his very identity as an Indian poet writing in English. More often than not, he is considered 'fake', not genuine enough to stand comparison with the 'authentic', *swadeshi* poet writing in the vernacular. He has been accused of "whoring after English Gods," desperately seeking inspiration from foreign poets. Would it be correct to dismiss the Indian English poet as a mere aberration or a luxury uncalled for in the Indian context?

Few Indian poets in English can be accused of not being self-conscious about their artistic identity. In fact, most of them suffer from an acute sense of literary self-consciousness all but preventing them from realizing or actualizing their full potential. They seem to suffer from 'a writer's block' defined as a psychological condition in which the writer is overawed by the predicament in which he finds himself:

My tongue in English chains,
I return, after a generation to you . . .
To live in Tamilnadu is to be conscious
everyday of impotence
There is the language, for instance:
The bull, Nammalvar took by the horns,
is today an unrecognizable carcass,
quick with the fleas of Kodambakkam. (Parthasarathy)

I have whistled for the Thames standing
on Ganga's bank . . .
I have traded my mangoes
for daffodils and my tongue has
found an alien grave. (C. Raju)

If Parthasarathy or Raju is trapped in a predicament involving an ambivalent allegiance to two different linguistic cultures, the rhetorical celebration of Kamala Das's emancipation fails to conceal her self-consciousness about the use of English in her poetry. She converts her uneasiness into a gesture of defiance which appears to suit her unconventional posture:

I am Indian, very brown, born in
Malabar, I speak three languages, write in
Two, dream in one. Don't write in English, they said,
English is not your mother tongue. Why not leave
Me alone, critics, friends, visiting cousins,
Every one of you? Why not let me speak in
Any language I like?

On the choice of the medium of English, several have expressed their reservations. There are those who refer to writers who started out with English and ended up writing in their mother tongue. There are others who speak of a productive tension between allegiance to English and love of the mother tongue. Poets like A.K. Ramanujan dismiss the whole question as not quite relevant. According to Ramanujan, the real question is related to the fact whether or not the poet is genuinely urged to communicate in English. If the force from within is genuine, no one can find fault with the choice of English. Or, as Rajan would suggest, if English is "the language of least compromise" for the writer, let him use it. Here there is no question of the mother tongue or the other tongue. It is the poet who should decide whether he is going to use English or any other. Let no one dictate what he should do or should not do.

The poet's self-consciousness is not limited to the choice of an alien tongue. In what literary tradition should he discover his poetic identity is another question which puzzles the poet. A history without a tradition, observed Parthasarathy, commenting on Indian poetry in English. There is neither a poet's poet nor a sustaining literary convention to fall back upon or to gain a foothold. Even in the case of a poet writing in the native tradition, "the conventions at his disposal do not lessen the agony of self-election; if he admires the ancients, he trembles to rival them; if he does not admire, he trembles before a void he must fill." (Hartman, *Beyond Formalism*) In the case of the Indo-English poet, he has to encounter a double challenge: his own literature and the past masters in English. How does he define his poetic identity vis-a-vis this double heritage? How does he embody his Indianness? Or should be just mind the business of writing only? Vilas Sarang wants him to be a Poet first. "Let the Poet be himself; by being himself, the poet, in fact, contributes to the definition of Indianness." (Vilas Sarang, *Indian English Poetry Since 1950*) Indianness as such cannot become a criterion of aesthetic value.

If the Romantic poet could not escape "the anxiety of influence" and "the burden of the past," can the Indian poet in English avoid being confronted with the question of "belatedness"? Heir to a culture reaching back to the Vedas and the Maha Kavyas of old, let alone Shakespeare and Milton and other moderns, how does he come to terms with this burden of the past? Writing in a language not his own, wouldn't he feel disinherited? Isn't he destined to be a 'fake' and hence a victim of 'writer's block'? The self-consciousness of the Indian poet in English needs to be understood not in terms of failure or lack of mastery but as a psychological condition challenging him to prove himself as poet. For example, like his English forbears, he is at once aware of the impossibility yet the necessity of being original. Those susceptible to this malady are the ones who lack a strong sense of being "genuine." It is a predicament which can be overcome only by a creative struggle to subdue if not subjugate the troubling impulses that prevent the poet from being spontaneous and natural. The very struggle with the medium or the predicament in which he is placed becomes an alibi for writing. In other words, he becomes his own subject matter. When we examine the Indian poet's writing in English, we are constantly made aware of the strain the poet is experiencing. Very rarely are we rewarded with the strength that the poet is capable of manifesting.

II

"It is in the English class room that the Indian Renaissance was born," wrote Gokak once. Whatever was the precise aim of Macaulay's Minute, it was to produce not just clerks to run a colonial empire. It was soon to produce a *clerisy* who assimilated the best in western culture and brought about a revolution at once political and cultural. That was the first Indian Renaissance which could balance tradition and modernity without endangering the basic Indian sensibility.

The clerisy who felt disinherited and compelled to cultivate a colonial sensibility have to once again claim their rightful place. Now more than ever do we feel the need to cultivate a bi-literary sensibility and awareness. "We do not live in a single matrix of culture." The contemporary man is a man of mixed allegiances. He is not the insular man but the cosmopolitan man. Art is becoming international today. 'Cosmopolitan' has become the very condition of modern art. Take the impact of technology, transport, multi-media etc. into consideration. A writer's formal or stylistic options are no longer limited to one's own cultural parameters. Hence the need to define one's self in the 'language of least compromise.' (Rajan)

The country is changing and changing very fast from an agrarian to an industrial society. Would the proverbial capacity for assimilation of which we are very proud be adequate to come to terms with the new? Wouldn't the impact of technology bring about a change in the fundamental character of the Indian psyche? "In creating an image of this challenge," says Rajan, "there is perhaps a part to be played by the man of mixed sensibility, caught between crossfires, whose own mind is a microcosm of what he seeks to convey."

The poet Parthasarathy refers to a productive tension between vernacular literatures and the Indian writing in English; how, over the years, one felt a growing relationship emerging between the two, a fruitful dialogue whose value lies outside the personal and the traditional, and reach out to the universal. He feels that Indo-English writing, especially poetry, has a two hundred year history without a tradition to back up its effort. It is in this context that the concept of an Indian literature whose foundations could be derived from Indian culture could be discussed. An attempt could be made to arrive at a true historical sense which can come to terms with the presence of the past and its relevance in our negotiations with the future. The English clerisy can become the true conscience keepers and the cultural barometers of the nation only when they relate themselves first to vernacular writing.

These disinherited poets, who are supposed to be 'whoring after English Gods,' are courageous enough to endure the consequences of their choice of English and seek to discover their identity in 'English chains,' in the 'language of least compromise.' Not for them is tradition a mustry heirloom handed down from generation to generation. One has to sweat and earn it for one's self. A true sense of history and tradition is born when the writer, missing his roots, starts looking for them or when he explores the difficulties involved in the quest for roots.

Despite the lack of a sustaining tradition and a set of received poetic conventions, poets like Ramanujan, Kolatkar, Mahapatra and others are trying to forge a new idiom which offers to blend and bind two distinct cultural traditions or, in other words, they are discovering their cultural past by making gnostic odyssesys into their past. We sense a fruitful interaction between their awareness of the demands of the medium and their awareness of the claims of the subject matter. Further, we see the Indian conventions of poetry insinuating themselves into the complex mosaic of images woven either about Murugan or Khandoba.

III

While speculating on the future of Indian English poetry, we would do well to welcome the contribution made by Indian poets writing in

English. There is no need to dismiss 'small scale reflections.' In any case, large scale reflections are out of fashion. Even if we encounter occasionally any such, they are not likely to be relevant to the times. Faced with the problem of defining his identity, announcing his identity in his own terms, the Indian English poet cannot but make use of irony and parody. Literary critics who have acted in the interest of institutionalization of classics have usually distrusted parody and relegated it to the literary basement. It is not surprising to find the 'run-of-the-mill' critic calling in question or suspecting the bona fides of an Indian English poet whose basic strength lies in an ironic mode of apprehension. We are yet to appreciate the distinguished poetry of recent times devoted to the theme of the crisis of faith. *Jejuri* is not the only example. We have the poems of Ramanujan and Mahapatra, hymns of Ezekiel, not to speak of really good pieces like "The Making of a God" by a young poet deservedly recommended for one of the Commonwealth Poetry prizes and the recent poem on "Kali" which won the Commonwealth Poetry prize. Indian English poetry has come a long way from either playing the sedulous ape to English masters or being overwhelmed by the rich legacy of the Indian past. Not only has the poet brought about a secularization of the sacred idiom in which the Indian poet was wont to refer to Gods and Goddesses, he has been able to put in perspective age-old beliefs, rituals and rites of passage of immemorial India and their relevance to contemporary times.

Let me illustrate with one example from Ramanujan's recent collection, *Second Sight*, and the poem is "Ecology." As in the other poems of Ramanujan, it would be difficult to decide whether this poem is about his mother or about his family or about the three red Champak trees giving allergy seasonally to a number of people in his family. In one single imaginative grasp, Ramanujan manages to suggest nature, human nature, family history, and the current concerns about the need to preserve the environment for the future. The paraphrasable substance of the poem may be given in the following manner: the poet persona, the son, is talking about his mother and the three trees in their courtyard. The three red Champak trees had burst into flower sending the mother into her first blinding migraine of the season. The son is angry; in fact he is in a rage that this should have happened once again. The mother would not consent to have the trees cut down as the trees, which are as old as herself, provide annual flower, basketfuls of them for their family gods and goddesses. The trees's intimate connection with the family ritual and seasonal migraine and the mother's sacral view of nature and her unwitting endorsement of ecological concerns relevant to the fate of the earth and the future of mankind – all these are effortlessly brought out without any straining after special effects. This is a typical Ramanujan poem which is distinctly Indian in attitude and flavour.

When I read a Ramanujan poem talking of the mother or the father or his several uncles and cousins, I do not feel conscious of the medium in which it is written. It looks so natural for this to be put in English. In the same fashion, when I read a very distinguished piece written in Telugu by a young writer in the distinctive idiom of his region, I am not at all conscious of the oddity of the dialect. The meaning comes through so well that you are rarely conscious of the strange dialect. Am I using a single standard of judgement here or am I being partial to the Indian poet in English? When I read Raja Rao's description of the Ganga or the Mysore Wedding, I am not conscious of the English in which it is put. When I read Telugu fiction of the best type, the same kind of unselfconscious response is made. If this is valid, why should we valorize the vernacular poet as superior or why should we denigrate the achievement of the Indian writer in English?

Family Relationships in Indo-English Poetry

PREMA NANDAKUMAR

Literature is refined social documentation. Shorn of the mid-day glare of facts and figures, chronological surveyings and the bitterness of real life, the essence of our living is made permanent by linking it to imaginative experience. Then is the real Truth made manifest. Ever since man began to go in for literary documentation, social history has not lacked vital inputs. In fact, for almost all the historical details of the ancient past, our most reliable guides have been great poems. The *Iliad* and the *Odyssey*, the *Ramayana* and the *Mahabharata*, *Chilappadikaram* and *Manimekalai* are priceless treasures that mirror our Greek, Aryan and Dravidian past with great accuracy. They are all intensely human documents that reveal a good deal about familial relationships. The sadly beautiful parting scene between Hector and Andromache, the fraternal love between Rama and his three brothers, the righteous anger of wifely chastity imaged in Kannagi are all familiar instances.

At the same time, there is never a one-sided view of the relationships projected by our ancients. We do come across the adulterous relationship between Paris and Helen, the fratricidal war between the Pandavas and the Kauravas, the tragedy of faithless Sali, mother of Aaputhran. Indeed, if we wish to have a total view of familial relationships then and now, we must go to the classics.

The loving togetherness of a husband and wife – total strangers hitherto – is one of the most astonishing wonders of human civilization. And how succinctly it is brought out by Chembulappeyalnirar of the Sangam period:

My mother and yours
Who were they?
My father and yours,
How were they related?
Me and yourself,
What paths did we traverse?
Loving hearts here
Have welded together
Like rain water
Fallen on red earth.

It was also realized even then that marital incompatibility was an evil one lived with in society. Hence Avvaiyar's famous advice:

It is wonderful to live together
With an understanding, chaste dame.
But if she cared not for bounds
Better take to asceticism.

Even after the modern age ushered in interviews, court cases and statistics to produce social history, literature remains the best reflector of reality. Among new literatures in India, the youngest is the corpus written in English. From the very beginning Indians writing in English have commented upon family relationships with high seriousness because the traditional heritage of India gives great importance to the family unit. Parents and children, husbands and wives, brothers and sisters, grandparents, uncles, aunts—there is an almost unbelievable nectarean love that flows through these relationships as documented by the first generation Indo-Anglians. One of the earliest poets was Govin Chunder Dutt whose pardonable pride in his gifted daughters and son—Aru, Toru and Abju—has found poetic recordation. Of Abju:

Most loving is my eldest, and I love him most;
  Almost a man in seeming, yet a child . . .

Aru is "pure and mild, as evening's early star" while Toru is

Puny and elf-like, with dishevelled tresses,
Self-willed and shy, ne'er heeding that I call,
Intent to pay her tenderest addresses
To bird and cat, – but most intelligent . . .

Accurate evaluations too. It is melancholic to realize that all the three died at a very young age, Toru herself was to give us two immortal poems on the heavenly childhood that came to an end too soon because of cruel fate. 'Sita' speaks of the ancient story as retold by Toru's mother in the garden:

But who is this fair lady? Not in vain
She weeps, – for lo! at every tear she sheds
Tears from three pairs of young eyes fall again
And bowed in sorrow are the three young heads.
It is an old, old story, and the lay
Which has evoked sad Sita from the past
Is by a mother sung . . . 'Tis hushed at last
And melts the picture from their sight away,
Yet they shall dream of it until the day!
When shall those children by their mother's side
Gather, ah me! as erst at eventide?

The cry of irreparable loss with which the poem closes is echoed in "The Casuarina Tree." The tree reminds Toru of the happier childhood days when she played in its shade with them:

O sweet companions, loved with love intense,
For your sakes shall the tree be ever dear!
Blent with your images, it shall arise
In memory, till the hot tears blind mine eyes!

The husband-wife relationship was also often a subject for these poets. Govin Chunder Dutt and Manmohan Ghose were loving husbands who blessed their life's companions through poetry. P. Seshadri's sonnet in memory of his dead wife is characteristic of such verse:

Which look of yours is graven on my breast?
    Is it the one, when, with that gentle smile
Of yours, you hail'd me with a kindly zest
    That evening? Or when we drove awhile
Beyond the town, in neighbour forest-shades,
    You wandered at the mighty wrecks of time
Scattered about those hallowed, silent shades?
    When bending on my latest book of rhyme
You wished to know each song? Or, when that night
    The full orbed moon aglow upon your face,
You gazed with rapture from the terraced height
    Upon the Ganges draped in dazzling rays?
Or when that morn you slowly said 'farewell',
Struggling with varied thoughts which seemed to swell?

Elsewhere one did hear a jarring note or two. The best known poem on this aspect of marital love is Sarojini Naidu's *The Temple: A Pilgrimage of Love*. A trilogy on the varying stormy phases of husband-wife relationship, it opens with the section, "The Gate of Delight." A year's separation introduces a chasm in their relationship leading to the wife's agony and hysteria in "The Menace of Love." The final section is "The Sanctuary" when a new life of togetherness begins as total surrender holds the key to understanding and deeper love:

Strangle my soul and fling it into the fire!
Why should my true love falter or fear or rebel?
Love, I am yours to lie in your breast like a flower,
Or burn like a weed for your sake in the flame of hell.

It is said that the situation presented in *The Temple* sonnets is based on a parallel experience of love, rejection and surrender that Sarojini went through in her married life. The family, of course, meant much to her and such surrender was paid by her willingly as a tribute to her happy motherhood, to her maternal pride recorded in lines weaving the significances of the names of her children, Jayasurya, Padmaja, Ranadheera and Lilamani. Thus Sarojini about Padmaja Naidu:

Lotus-maiden, you who claim
All the sweetness of your name,
Lakshmi, fortune's queen, defend you . . .
Lotus-maiden, may you be
Fragrant of all ecstasy.

The problems experienced by Sarojini in her married life were the harbingers of further trouble to the Indian family unit because of the large-scale participation by women in our freedom struggle. Presently freedom came, but no peace for the family. Modern times in the West blew a strong breeze into our traditional patterns upsetting many settled usages. The last fifty years have been a period of impossible strain on our family life, a point excellently documented by the Tamil novelist Sivasankari in her *Palangal*. The joint family system is gone. Western education with its overdoing of the equality image has upset traditional checks and balances like filial obedience and parental responsibility. These changes are sharply etched in the English poetry written by Indians. But though we are willing to rebel, we are not too ready to put the thought into action. Inhibitions are frowned at bravely, but very few of us are ready to cross the magic line of tradition. As a result, an ambivalence has crept in our attitudes.

It is true that an overwhelming amount of English poetry is published in India throughout the year. All the same, very few poets are really concerned with the gigantic problems faced by man living in an increasingly poisoned earth which is poised perilously on the brink of a nuclear disaster. Most of the poets exhibit only conventional jottings of extramarital man-woman relationship. But almost all of them reserve a lyric or two for some aspect of one's familial life as if to prove that they do have some faith in their roots. Often it is in the shape of childhood memories. Again, a few writers do put in a footnote on husband-wife relationship or the miracle of parenthood. What is surprising is that even this tiny fraction (albeit repetitive) turns out to be a fair mass of familial poetry that has undeniable sociological relevance.

Traditionally Indians are committed to respect their parents. The *mathru devo bhava* injunction has been deeply embedded in the Indian psyche as may be noticed in Indo-English poetry. Even a random sampling shows the deep respect and love that the word 'mother' evokes. Such is Hemant Kulkarni's *pitripooja* in *Burning with a Smile* (1982):

I remember
mother telling me
of her delight
when she was pregnant with me:
Every evening she lighted a lamp
on the altar of God
and prayed for a light inside me
as I was growing
into brain and heart
to be ready for the world.

I have felt that inner light
all my life
knowing it to be
my mother's gift.
If my body and mind
dissolve into a shadow
that light would always abide.

Even in loving homages, other voices do creep in. Dom Moraes's attitude towards his mother is suggestive of the sorrow due to her mental breakdown and the image of his maimed motherland blends with that of his real mother:

Your eyes are like mine.
When I last looked in them
I saw my whole country,
A defeated dream
Hiding itself in prayers,
A population of corpses . . .

Sorrow has stopped your eye.
Your dream is desolate.
It calls me every day

But I will not enter it . . .
Forgive me my trespasses.

A like ironic distancing is Keki Daruwalla's approach:

Your memories flounder
amongst your sons now
you confuse the one who
wet his bed
with the one who
    bit through your dugs
    and made them septic

Parents are ubiquitous presences in the works of poets like A.K. Ramanujan (*Relations: Poems*, 1972), R. Rajeswar Upadhyaya (*Faking Realities*, 1964), Imtiaz Dharker (*Purdah*, 1988) and Hemant Kulkarni (*Burning with a Smile*, 1982). Mostly the sentiment is predictable: gratitude for a happier, care-free childhood.

There are startling messages of bitter truth that do strike us now and again. Nar Deo Sharma's "Letter from a Lost Daughter" (*Melody of Wounds*, 1984) is a sheer cry of anguish to turn the focus on struggling parents who try to get them married into a comfortable household:

Until I die my mother will
Remain pregnant with worries.
From the diary of your grief
Papa I dug out the truth that
God drowned in your lonely tears.

I can't forget the agonizing memory
Of your skeletal, blistered struggle
For me in the quest of
A well-paid, educated man who
Rated beyond your poor dreams . . .

I have removed your bier of worries:
Let me face the hard world alone.

While there are these grating voices, motherhood itself is looked upon with proper pride by Christine Gomez in "To be a Mother" (*Yatra*, 1989) and Yajna Sri Nambiar offers an Indian girl's defiant reply of love in "An Unseen Poem" (*Yatra*, 1989) to Sylvia Plath's desecratory Occidental filial hate in "Daddy." Unlike Sylvia's verbal assassination of the father, Yajna Sri is truly a daughter of Ind:

I am ineffectual –
To my father.
I am an Arjuna
To my father's Janardhana.
But Krishna was the charioteer
Who with compassion
Proved to Dhananjaya where he failed.
He loved him not the less
For his weakness.

The birth of a son causes termless wonder too. Shiv Kumar's cerebral phraseology is not devoid of a certain charm as he welcomes this "third traveller on the road to Emmaus" into his home in *Woodpeckers* (1979). A.V.S. Sarma can produce likable jingles for his son (Sarma, like Kumar is also a Professor of English) in *Revelations* (1982).

Despite a certain thematic overindulgence with love (or lust) outside the knot of matrimony, the family idea is very much with Indian poets in English. Even when they have alienated themselves from the families either by marriage or exile, an occasional family reunion is welcomed with pleasure albeit couched in ironic phraseology. R. Parthasarathy's "Homecoming" (*Rough Passage*, 1977) celebrates a reunion (probably during a typical Tirupati wedding) made up of childhood remembrances:

each one pulled,
Sitting cross-legged on the steps

of the choultry, familiar coconuts
out of the fire
of rice-and-pickle afternoons.

When we move to maturer years in one's life, there is a marked difference of tone. The passion of pre-independence days becomes rarer. Marital relationship is watched with ironic eyes and castigated often as a mechanical contraption set up by tradition. Rina Sodhi's "Indian Woman" (*Selected Poems*, 1981) is so typical:

Love
comes like nausea
to an Indian woman
she sights
she groans
Marriage
is arranged
more sighs
more groans
Motherhood
is unplanned
she spreads
like jungle fire
from the flesh
to the bones
Life
is a matter
of 591 milestones
285 sighs
286 groans.

Nissim Ezekiel, however, finds wedded love passion enough in "Marriage Poem" (*Collected Poems*, 1989):

Between the acts of wedded love
A quieter passion flows,
Which keeps the nuptial pattern firm
As passion comes and goes,
And in the soil of wedded love
Rears a white rose

Some poets give importance to intellectual companionship which is much stronger than mere platonic love. Rabindranath Menon's "Letter from a Divorcee" (*Pebbles on the Shore*, 1981) dissects the several steps of marital incompatibility:

Marriage couldn't be a
union of hearts alone for those
with heads. Intellect must be equally close.

But when there is a union of hearts nothing can really come in between, asserts Ashok Mahajan in "Partners" (*Vivisections*, 1980):

The bride
Possessed no trousseau
Save her tresses.
Her groom's wages were
A wad of words.
Yet they showered
Their meagre gifts
Upon each other
Like confetti. . . .

Such monsoon-fling of youth
Left them legacies.
Aging together, they watch
Both fungus and the algae grow
As lichens upon their hyetal tree
In rich symbiosis now.

In any case, more often than not, even if beaten the Indian wife (mostly the rural variety, though) would rather stand by her husband against interfering (even if well-meaning) strangers, ruefully exclaims Polanki Ramamoorthy in *Rangoli* (1985):

Who the hell are you?
How dare you raise your hand on my man?
He is my husband –

why shouldn't he beat me –
but who the blasted hell are you?

It is hard to come by a poetess dissecting her husband but Kamala Das rises to the challenge in the anthology piece, "The Stone Age," which is actually an embarrassing ode to adultery:

Fond husband, ancient settler in the mind,
Old fat spider, weaving webs of bewilderment,
Be kind. You turn me into a bird of stone, a granite
Dove, you build round me a shabby drawing room,
And stroke my pitted face absent-mindedly while
You read. With loud talk you bruise my pre-morning sleep
You stick a finger into my dreaming eye.

Quite a few men pay extravagant tributes to their life-partners. In fact Adiyar's *Wife* (1987) is a sumptuous exercise that sings paens to her who is a willing slave:

But my wife . . .
Has shackled me with the Thali
Around my legs
Keeps me on the pedestal
Of her sanctuary.

It is rather strange that brothers and sisters are not considered in Indo-English poetry these days. Probably the nuclear family has made this a distant past now. One vainly searches for a poem like Toru's *Sita* in these volumes. An occasional exception certainly brightens our day. Eugene d'Vaz's "Two Little Brothers" (*The Fire Rose*, 1981) exquisitely recaptures the early dawn of brotherly togetherness which vanishes in the harsh midday sun of middle age. It is a paradisal image which can be seen only in one's memory:

I was once like you.
Now my intentions are muddled.
The world threw faggots and boulders
On our way

Till our days got fouled
Till the wind stopped singing and howled.
He goes his way, I mine.
And 'Brother' is just another
Of those stupid words.

Once we enter this territory of family relationships in Indo-English poetry, a staggering amount of material gets piled up begging us for statistical analysis and critical commentary on the emerging trends. For, it is not only parents, husbands, wives, and children who people this world. There are also cousins and aunts, uncles and in-laws. And grandparents. Grandparents viewed as curmudgeonish crones by poets like Ashok Mahajan or remembered with understanding pity as in Jayanta Mahapatra's well-known poem "Grandfather" (*Life Signs*, 1983) on Chintamani Mahapatra who embraced Christiánity during the terrible Orissa famine of 1866 since he was starving and on the point of death:

We wish we knew what it was to be, against dying,
to know the dignity
that had to be earned dangerously,
your last chance that was blindly terrifying, so unfair.
We wish we had not to wake up with our smiles
in the middle of some social order.

God's plenty here. And if we added up K.R. Srinivasa Iyengar's epic, *Sitayana* (1987) to the corpus, we have a whole view of ideal family life. For *Sitayana* exhaustively presents Sita as a daughter, sister, daughter-in-law, wife and mother. In spite of all the sorrows and exile, there is no sense of alienation in Iyengar's Sita for she is capable of being very much an individual and at the same time ably interweaves herself as part of the larger web of life.

She was conscious all her yesteryears found
    their meaning in the present,
which in its turn forged its seminal links
    with all that's yet to be born.

Here on the left, the past, and its tally
    of fulfilments and failures;
and here on the right, the unborn future:
    the present justifies all.

And so Maithili, tired but contented,
    rested in peace for awhile.
and now refreshed and happy, was ready
    for the tasks of motherhood.

It is heartening that the Indo-English poet doesn't shy away from experimenting with any compound in human experience and is right now documenting the social truth about the Indian family which may prove to be of great poetic, historical and sociological interest in the 21st century.

Sri Aurobindo's *Savitri*: The Vision and the Prophecy

D.V.K. RAGHAVACHARYULU

Sri Aurobindo's *Savitri* is "a story long written but acted now." It is a Maha-Kavya which embodies a visionary response to the compelling need of our times to discover for modern man a more meaningful sense of life in the cosmic order than his present situation and view of human destiny can afford. Contemporary literature, both western and Indian, has come to be predominantly negative in projecting the human condition. It sounds like a dirge sung mournfully to the futility, despair and the tragedy of man bent on self-destruction and universal annihilation. Among the modern classics of despair, like T.S. Eliot's *The Waste Land*, Kafka's *The Castle*, Camus's *The Outsider*, Bellow's *Mr. Sammler's Planet*, Naipaul's *Guerrillas* and Salman Rushdie's *Midnight's Children*, there is at work the punitive logic of reality rather than the affirming grace of faith. It is in such a context that one turns to a refreshingly different attitude to man and his place in the scheme of things, which is reflected in Indian masterpieces like Tagore's *Gitanjali*, Prasad's *Kamayani* and Sri Aurobindo's *Savitri*. In these great poems, we have human transcripts that celebrate man's transcendence of existential limitation and his ultimate evolution towards higher places of consciousness linking him to the eternal verities.

The progressive secularization of poetry in our times has rendered religious and spiritual themes unfashionable and suspect. Hence the resistance of modern critical opinion to such "raids on the inarticulate" as are not amenable to the naturalistic and ironic modes of intellectual response. However, there is a point at which poetry becomes important, not because it is art, but because it is a passionate outcry for more life, a greater intensity of feeling, and a higher realization of consciousness. Beyond man's material, aesthetic, intellectual and existential needs, there are also his spiritual needs, the needs of the soul to be fulfilled. It is exactly these needs that are met by the poetry of faith, and Sri Aurobindo's *Savitri*, an epic of human possibility, is the most impressive achievement of a poetic imagination, "which is nothing less than God as He operates in the human soul."

Sri Aurobindo's *Savitri* has behind it a long tradition as well as a background of personal evolution. A completely western-oriented gentleman, almost de-Indianized before returning to India after staying too long in the West, Sri Aurobindo was twice-born in the throes of the Indian renaissance, mastering an India rediscovered through her usable past and her timeless aspiration. Later he plunged himself into nationalist politics, a fierce radical and activist, only to realize soon that his real role lay elsewhere, beyond the clamour of public affairs. When he left for Pondicherry to turn into a man of God, he was impelled by a vision of India as the spiritual genetrix of the world, a role from which she had been cut off by historical contingency, but a role which she was nevertheless bound to resume and fulfill in the earnest of time. Far from retiring from the world-scene, Sri Aurobindo had re-entered the more purposive realm of the spiritual regeneration of mankind. He viewed life as a Purna-Yoga, an ultimate consonance of Truth, Service and God-realization, culminating in the Advent of the Life Divine. In fact, his whole life at Pondicherry, from 1910 to 1950, was a pattern of ceaseless Sadhana aimed at preparing the soil of India as the seed-bed of the Future Man and a comprehensive flowering of human promise.

Since *Savitri* was intended to be a poetic testament of Sri Aurobindo's concept of the Life Divine, a work in which poetry aspires to the condition of prayer,—"half a prayer from below, and half a whisper from above, whisper and prayer chiming into song"—and a litany addressed to the Mother of the Universe, we may pay some attention to the core ideas of Aurobindonian philosophy that are embedded in it. Sri Aurobindo held the belief that the process of evolution is continuous, forward-looking and directed towards higher forms of consciousness leading to an ultimate unity with the Divine. Even as matter evolved into life, and life thrust itself forward to mind, mind too must generate the supermind or the oversoul. The limitation, relativity and ambivalence in the historical and existential world of man, giving rise to ignorance, falsehood and evil, and resulting in pain, suffering and violence, are the manifestations of an evolution which is now partial, incomplete and unfulfilled. Once consciousness rises above mere sensibility and intellection, the pattern of unity amid diversity can be clearly perceived and Earth-Life and Cosmic Being stand wedded to a common purpose. As Dante says:

> All, as I name them, down from leaf to leaf,
> Are in gradation throned on the Rose.

Another cardinal idea was that existence consists of two movements: the downward descent from perfect wholeness (Brahman) towards matter representing the disparate unity of life; and the upward ascent from matter and mind and supermind to wholeness (Sachidananda). Attaining the still centre of the Divine implies the experience of these two movements, which in their collaboration, potentiate the evolutionary dynamic towards a cosmic alliance of Life, Nature and God. Man's striving and the avataric intercession of the Divine combined to alleviate and redeem humanity from nescience, inconscience and impercipience which lie at the root of all misery, anxiety and sorrow. Death, which strikes terror into the human soul and distracts the consciousness and begets discord and violence in human affairs, is but the shadow cast on life by the higher life. If life is beyonded by death, death too can be beyonded by life; for in the life eternal the quick and the dead stand mutually related to the Absolute on which evolution has a momentary lien in the temporal world.

The conquest of Death is the thematic nexus of Sri Aurobindo's *Savitri*. In his earlier poems, *Urvasie* and *Love and Death*, Sri Aurobindo presents the principle of love as not only triumphing over death, but also embracing it in the magnificence of recovered life. In *Ahana*, he goes beyond the romantic solution and hints at a higher power of love, operating through the divine Grace, symbolized by dawn, which brings about a spiritual transformation of the soul exceeding Knowledge, Power and Joy, and the annunciation of a celestialized earth.

> Someday surely
> The world too shall be saved from death by love.

In *Thought the Paraclete* and *The Rose of God*, the aspiring soul intones the flame-word rune in its mystic communion with the divine, the empowering creative passion of Love.

In *Savitri*, the theme of love is broadened and deepened, and identified with the circumambient love of God for his creation. The assurance of the advent of the Life Divine is held out as the promise and hope of man's redemption from the earthly life bedevilled by strife, division, ignorance, hatred and violence. In transforming the ancient *Mahabharata* tale of Savitri from legend to symbol, Sri Aurobindo shapes a new myth and vision responsive and answerable to the modern human predicament.

While Savitri in the original version succeeds in winning back Satyavan from death to life by the virtue of her chastity aided by a romantic coup of feminine resourcefulness which disarms the chivalrously absent-minded Yama, Sri Aurobindo's Savitri achieves her victory over death by the exertion of the cosmic will and soul-force in the fields of evolving human consciousness at the highest level at which Yama himself is revealed as a functionary and promoter of life.

> My will is greater than thy law, O Death;
> My love is stronger than the bonds of Fate.

Thus the main thrust of Sri Aurobindo's *Savitri* is to present the heroine as a bearer of prevenient grace into a world afflicted and crippled by mortality and hew the ways of immortality as a spiritual pioneer, pilgrim and redeemer. We are indebted to God as Emily Dickinson says, not so much for oxygen, but for electricity, more for light than for life. In rendering this theme, Sri Aurobindo imposes a new structure and architectonic on the old narrative, shifting its emphasis from the episodic to the epic dimension, and informing its content with a new vision and prophecy, declaring Eternity as an event.

Savitri is an immense work comprising 3 parts, 12 books, 49 cantos, and 24,000 lines of sustained incandescence, intensity and grandeur. In spite of its intimidating bulk and mystic burden, the poem has a luminous simplicity of structure and import. The action of the poem is presented in *media res*, with the fateful dawn of the day Satyavan must die.

That was the hour before the gods awake. Dawn is everywhere; but earth turning on itself misses it by halves; Eternity is always, but time misses it in the flow of moments; Truth is omnipresent, but the mind misses it in its evanescent routes of thought. The birth of Ushas represents symbolically the three generic movements of Light, Knowledge and Immortality. By implication and suggestion, it also shows that ignorance is incompletion, death is but ungained life, and darkness is absent light, the force of apparent negation that press upon the human condition of which Satyavan as Everyman is the hostage. Savitri in her double role as human and divine is presented as the anagogic individual who must transform the mortal twilight into the Greater Dawn through her soul-force. In her the mental, vital and spiritual horizons of Being unite to converge upon the unhorizoned Absolute.

To this end Aswapathy's own immense journey into the various occult worlds is made consonant. Savitri is his Yagna-Phala, for his prayers and supplications to the Universal Mother are answered by her Avataric descent into the earth-fold. Aswapathy's Sadhana proceeds on three levels: to attain spiritual fulfilment as an individual; to gain transcendence and expansion of consciousness as a typical representative of the human race; and to seek and implore the gifts of the Divine for all Creation. As a witness self and altruistic beyonder, he communicates his vision of the children of a new dawn:

> I saw the Omnipotent's flaming pioneers
> Over the heavenly verge which turns towards life
> Come crowding down the amber stairs of birth. . . .
>
> The sun-eyed children of a marvellous dawn
> The great creators with wide brows of calm,
> The massive barrier breakers of the world. . . .
>
> The architects of immortality. . . .
> Their tread one day shall change the suffering earth
> And justify the light on Nature's face.

Sage Narada, who foresees the human side of Savitri's marriage to Satyavan, explains to the Queen-Mother that pain is the hammer with which the gods chisel and sculpt mortal substance into immortal form, also forecasts Savitri's saviour role, and the battle she must wage in order to realize her ordained goal.

> No human aid can reach her in that hour,
> No armed God stand shining at her side.
> Cry not to heaven, for she alone can save
> For this silent Force came missioned down;
> In her the conscious will took human shape:
> She only can save herself and save the world.

Thus the narrative turns upon Savitri's courtship, wedded happiness, and her *Triratra* Penance, climaxing into the primal confrontation with Yama, the God of Death. Savitri's Sadhana takes her through the regions beyond the presiding Madonnas of Sorrow, Might and Light, and in the vast expansion of consciousness which takes place in her, the radiance, harmony and the creative dynamism of the Divine hold out the assurance of Eternal Life and of Earth-Transformation. In this afflatus of spiritual illumination, Yama is no longer the terrible dark god, but he becomes a revenant of the Life Divine, wooing creation from above. At first, he bore "the deep pity of destroying gods, with brows of unwearying calm large godlike lids, Silent upheld the writhing serpent, Life." But anon, in Savitri's self-vastation, as the Divine Mother, he is himself transformed.

> His being like a huge fort of darkness towered,
> Around it her life grew, an ocean's siege;
> Light like a turning tongue licked up his thoughts,
> Light was a luminous torture in his heart,
> Light coursed, a splendid agony through his nerves;
> His darkness muttered perishing in her blaze.
> Her mastering word commanded every limb
> And left no room for his enormous will. . . .
>
> He called to Night but she fell shuddering back;
> He called to Hell but sullenly it retired;
> Afar he fled shunning her dreaded touch
> And refuge took in the retreating Night.

With Yama, thus subdued and overpowered by Savitri's godhead, Death appears transfigured in the light of Everlasting Day:

> One whom her soul had faced as Death and Night
> A sum of all sweetness gathered into his limbs
> And blinded her heart to the beauty of the suns.

Satyavan is restored and united to Savitri, but now to gather all creation towards a joyous destiny:

> Thy energy, Lord, to seize on woman and man,
> To take all things and creatures in their grief
> And gather them into a mother's arm.

The magic flowing waters of deep love enchafe the earth and swirl is on towards a mighty hymn of adoration. The Divine Logos, addressing Savitri as the vedic Sun-Word, or Gayatri, entitles her to a hitherto unattempted cosmic heroism and power and glory:

> When all thy work in human Time is done,
> The mind of earth shall be a home of light,
> The life of earth a tree growing towards heaven,
> The body of earth a tabernacle of God.

Savitri, the poem, thus ends on the note of a gesturing intimation of a greater, more supernal dawn, and the symbolic action comes full circle:

> Night, splendid with the moon dreaming in heaven
> In silver peace, possessed her luminous reign.
> She brooded through her stillness on a thought
> Deep-guarded by her mystic folds of light,
> And in her bosom nursed on a greater Dawn.

Sri Aurobindo's *Savitri* is in a sense a modern allegory of Love, a Divine Comedy, in which the power of Love evolving from Eros to Psyche and from Agape to Caritas, merges with the Grace and Bliss of God. The Love Divine rescues and redeems the suffering soul of Man and directs the Life-Force from the fiasco of mortality towards the Fiesta of Immortality. In communicating the rapture and ecstasy of the mystic experience which permeates the poem's aesthetic inscape, Sri Aurobindo combines the narrative, apocalyptic and prophetic voices into a mantric idiom dramatizing the triune incantation of the ancient Gayatri litany. He also invests the poem with a quality of sublimity, which, in the words of A.C. Bradley, is "derived from the overwhelming greatness of power" that the ancient legend acquires its symbolic shape and semantics. The symbol Dawn, with which the poem opens, is a splendid exemplification of Sri Aurobindo's prophetic vision doubled into the poetics of Epiphany, in which image and symbol, tone and tenor, and imagination and intuition all merge and unite into a Yogic invocation of the Vedic Dawn:

> A wandering hand of pale enchanted light
> That glowed along a fading moment's brink,
> Fixed with gold panel and opalescent hinge
> A gate of dreams ajar on mystery's verge.
> One lucent corner windowing hidden things
> Forced the world's blind immensity to sight.
> The darkness failed and slipped like a falling cloak
> From the reclining body of God.
> Then through the pallid rift that seemed at first
> Hardly enough for a trickle from the Suns,
> Outpoured the revelation and the Flame.

Sri Aurobindo believed that poetic utterance, at its overhead levels, partakes of the aesthesis of the soul and is, at its highest, inseparable from Divine Logos: *Raso Vai Sah*. Viewed in this light, *Savitri* need not be distanced or marginalized as an esoteric masterpiece for the erudite few, but acknowledged and approached as a spiritual classic for all, bringing nectarean delight even to the common reader.

The Chessmaster and His Moves: A Review of Reviews and an Introduction

MAKARAND R. PARANJAPE

In this paper I propose to do three things: first to uncover certain interpretative cruxes in *Chessmaster* through a discussion of the reception of the book in India. Secondly, to touch on what might be termed Raja Rao's larger ideological project and, thus, to lead up to a preliminary interpretation of the text. And, finally, to offer what I consider to be three useful approaches which can further help to untangle the text.

I

Raja Rao's widely-awaited magnum opus, *The Chessmaster and His Moves*, was finally released in June 1988. The story of its publication is, by no means, commonplace. The book had taken over ten years to write and the manuscript had been ready at least five years before its actual publication. More than one major American publisher had shown interest in the manuscript, but considered the book too long. Viking suggested a reduction to a third of its present size of 735 pages. And what is even more amazing is that the ms. being shown around was merely the first part of a projected trilogy! Raja Rao refused to cut down on his book. Subsequently, Vision Books of Delhi, the pioneers of the paperback business in India, whose earlier imprints, Hind Pocket Books and Orient Paperbacks, had published nearly every major contemporary Indian author either in original English or in English translation, accepted the book as it was. The publisher took over three years to finally publish the book. As it happened, when the proofs of the book were ready, Raja Rao suddenly became one of the contenders for the prestigious Neustadt Prize awarded by the University of Oklahoma. The xerox copies of the proofs were circulated among members of the jury. Raja Rao did win the prize, which was awarded to him on 4 June, 1988. And shortly thereafter, the book was formally released in India.[1]

Raja Rao, everybody would acknowledge, is one of the three leading Indian English novelists; the other two are Mulk Raj Anand and R.K. Narayan. Furthermore, going by the number of critical studies on it, his *Serpent and the Rope* (1960) has the best claims to be considered the single most influential and accomplished of Indian English novels. I can think of no other contenders to this title except G.V. Desani's *All About H. Hatterr* (1948) or Salman Rushdie's *Midnight's Children* (1983). Yet, the former has not attracted the kind of attention that *The Serpent and the Rope* did, while the latter's reputation has yet to stabilize. After *The Serpent and the Rope*, Raja Rao published only two books, the highly-acclaimed *The Cat and Shakespeare* (1965) and the disappointing *Comrade Kirillov* (1976). *Kirillov* had appeared in a French version much earlier, in 1965. Hence, *Chessmaster* appeared twenty-eight years after Raja Rao's last major book, *The Serpent and the Rope*, and twenty-five years after the other two books. The appearance of *Chessmaster* was certainly a major literary event in the world of Indian English literature. Much anticipation had been built up by the long years of silence and the recent award of the Neustadt Prize had added to the excitement of those waiting for the book's release. To say the least, everybody expected something big – at last, the *great* Indian English novel!

At the outset I must clarify that in the following story of the reception of *Chessmaster*, I shall be concerned primarily with its reception in India. Hence, I leave out of my discussion the two essays by R. Parthasarathy, "*The Chessmaster and His Moves*: The Novel as Metaphysics," and Edwin Thumboo, "Raja Rao: *The Chessmaster and His Moves*" in *World Literature Today* (Autumn 1989, 561-66, 567-73). This number was specially prepared to felicitate Raja Rao as the winner of the Neustadt Prize for 1988. It was published towards the end of 1988 and reached India only around March or April 1989. By then, all the reviews that I shall discuss had already appeared in India. The articles it contains were specially commissioned for this purpose and therefore belong, in proper, to a period prior to the general release of the book. Both Parthasarathy's and Thumboo's essays are useful as general introductions to the book and both stress its philosophical backgrounds. Parthasarathy's essay contains a survey of Raja Rao's earlier work, notes on philosophical sources of the book, and on some of its leading characters. It is neither an interpretation, nor a coherent reading of the novel. Thumboo's essay is more detailed and discusses the central philosophical issue in the novel, which he identifies as the quest for the Absolute. This essay also contains valuable insights into Raja Rao's characterization and narrative technique. Despite the fact that all the essays in this volume were commissioned, the occasional note of irritation cannot help creeping into some of them. Uma Parmeswaran, for instance, complains:

> Raja Rao the thinker seems a male chauvinist who identifies masculine sensibility with the male gender and feminine sensibility with the female gender and has carried this to such an extent in his latest novel that it seems to be an insufferable heap of chauvinistic pomposity in which, moreover, all the literary flaws of his earlier novels – split plots, slow action, weak narrative devices such as diary entries, and imbalanced characterization – appear in a magnified form. . . . Rao seems to have stretched out his recent novel into an endless ream of words so as to prevent even the most patient of readers from finding out that the core is just a hollow echo of his masterpieces of earlier years. (569-70)

Parmeswaran's comments are in consonance with those of several Indian readers of the novel. Apart from this special issue, to my knowledge as of July 1989, the book has not been reviewed anywhere else in the Western press.

Therefore, let me proceed directly to the book's reception in India. Soon after its release in June, publicity copies were sent out to the major periodicals. By August authorized excerpts and reviews started appearing in the Indian press. *The Illustrated Weekly of India* and *The Sunday Standard* carried excerpts, but no reviews. To the best of my knowledge, the first review that appeared was by Girija Kumar in the Sunday *National Herald*, 7 August 1988. The headline caption hailed the book as "A Major Work," and overall the review was positive. Yet

Kumar acknowledged that the book was "difficult to read": its narrative "is not like a river in full flow, but like a sluggish stream meandering through shallow waters of numerous lagoons on the way to its ultimate destination." Kumar's review, however, made one extremely valuable point about Raja Rao's philosophical method in the book:

> Everything is ultimately reduced to mathematical equations and indeed all gods are said to be mathematical formulate [sic].

This statement shows a glimmer of the recognition of what I consider to be one of the most important techniques of the book. I shall come back to this point later.

Prolixity, tediousness, and repetitiousness – such charges have been made by many subsequent readers of the book, among them some of our leading Indian English critics. In a review which appeared in the Sunday edition of *The Tribune* on 28 August, K.S. Duggal said that Raja Rao's philosophical disquisitions, at times, "could be eliminated without injury to the action of the story." In a more influential review for *Indian Literature* (No. 130, March-April 1989), M.K. Naik, after unfavourably comparing *Chessmaster* with *The Serpent and the Rope*, accuses the novel of possessing "neither a solid thematic core nor a taut narrative" and of "general vagueness and confusion, drift and lack of precision." (177) A major critic of Indian English fiction told me that she turned down the offer to review the book for the pre-eminent fortnightly, *India Today*, because she found it too long and unreadable. One of our senior-most critics and a long-standing champion of Raja Rao confessed to me that he found the book too long, and unnecessarily repetitious. Another leading academic of considerable authority quipped that reading the novel was like "walking in ointment."[2]

But it was the second review of the book by Prema Nandakumar for the venerable South Indian paper, *The Hindu*, published on 23 August 1989, that really blew the lid off such more or less guarded criticism. Nandakumar's piece, entitled "Polite passion of the bourgeois drawing room," is characterized by biting sarcasm and measured scorn. The review begins with a series of questions:

> Are we creating an age of false taste by championing with excessive zeal the cause of Raja Rao? Is he a Vedantic philosopher or

an insufferable poseur? Is he the standard-bearer of the genuine Indian English style or the wrecker of the pliant language's spiritual possibilities.

The review goes on to show, in a tellingly Tamil comparison, how much the *Chessmaster* is really a rewriting of *The Serpent and the Rope*: "Old tamarind rice in new polythene bags." This is certainly an important point which was later picked up by Naik as well. What makes Nandakumar's attack so damaging is that she implies that Raja Rao is a hypocrite, a fraud. Moreover, Nandakumar debunks Raja Rao's celebrated style, with its long sentences and multilingual erudition. About the latter she says:

> Transliterated chinks from various languages are strewn around like undigested pieces of food in a gourmet's innards, and Raja Rao goes on and on mesmerised by his own voices[.]

Also, Nandakumar is put off by what she considers the book's weepy sentimentality that hints at a larger decadence. She reacts to "Desecratory images like copulation beneath the portraits of Sarada Devi and Ramakrishna Paramahamsa." Overall, the review is a sweeping indictment of Raja Rao.

Among the reviews that appeared in the Indian press, only one more remains to be discussed. This is by G.S. Amur, another respected critic and scholar. Published in the Sunday edition of *The Deccan Herald* on 9 October, the review is entitled, "Cosmic game that life is." Amur's review is different because he takes the book seriously and focuses on a major preoccupation of the novel, the dialectic between zero and infinity:

> Raja Rao's novels derive their structure from a dialectic between two levels of presentation, one operating horizontally and dealing with events in time and space and the other operating vertically through a celebration of truths transcending these dimensions.

The review ends abruptly, owing perhaps to the editor's scissors, and we are left without Amur's evaluation of the novel.

The last item to appear on the book was written under the byline of Shiv K. Kumar, an important writer and critic; however, it is not really a review but a report on the Neustadt Prize. It was published in the Sunday Magazine of *The Hindustan Times* on 4 December 1988. Just one more comment, again negative, probably directed at the book, appeared in Khushwant Singh's famous column, "With Malice towards One and All" (*The Deccan Chronicle*, 24 July 1989):

> There is also a strong element of narcissism in Raja Rao's long novels in which he barely conceals his identity as the handsome guru delivering sermons to his nubile *chelis* [female disciples] who in turn gratefully offer him all they have – *tan* (body), *man* (mind) and *dhan* (worldly wealth). Such nauseating self-esteem is mercifully absent in his short stories.

Singh is probably making a dig at Sivarama Sastri's relations with the four women in his life, Jayalakshmi, Suzanne, Mireille, and Uma – all of whom he charms with his intellect and who are devoted to him. Uma, of course, is his step-sister, with whom Siva has a strong sensual, though not sexual, bond.

And after that there has been a deafening silence. The book appears to have sunk without a ripple. Just five reviews and a couple of more reports and excerpts for such an important book? Surely such a response is symptomatic of a larger problem that readers have with the work of Raja Rao.

I would not go to the extent of saying the *Chessmaster* has polarized the Indian English critical community into those who can't stand Raja Rao and those who love him; certainly, few of the latter group have come out in support of the book. But I am going to argue that *Chessmaster*, by being such extreme example of a Raja Rao text, has highlighted certain problems as never before. Some of these problems were identified within a year of the publication of *The Serpent and the Rope* in a review by David McCutchion called, "The Novel as Shastra."[3] I would like to go back to this essay briefly because I consider it to be one of the best ever written on Raja Rao's work. McCutchion starts with a Kiplingesque assertion:

> The whole idea that the great Indian novel is somehow going to 'reconcile' or 'assimilate' East and West is strangely misconceived, because the two approaches to life (and it is the approach that determines whether the novel is 'Indian' or 'English') are mutually exclusive. (90)

McCutchion stresses the incommensurality of the Indian and the Western paradigms of reality. The question is, of course, whether this is true empirically or whether such antithetical constructions are ideological. This question assumes importance because Raja Rao himself is preoccupied with it. I shall discuss his answers, which are surprisingly identical to McCutchion's, though framed differently, later. But what McCutchion seems to be questioning is the whole philosophy of synthesis and reconciliation between two systems which are, to him, totally incompatible:

> Considering that the novel's chief concern is circumstantial reality . . . and that the traditional Indian viewpoint regards all this as tedious illusion, it may be questioned whether a truly Indian novel is at all possible. Raja Rao's book makes no attempt at half way solutions taking the 'best' of both worlds: its sensibility and values are uncompromisingly Indian, absorbing all experience from the point of view of one who seeks Brahman. (90)

McCutchion's identification of Indian tradition with a particular permutation of a particular philosophical system is questionable, so is his definition of the novel as a work whose chief concern is "circumstantial reality." Also questionable is his assumption that somebody who seeks Brahman, as Raja Rao's protagonists ostensibly do, cannot be concerned with circumstantial reality. In fact, Raja Rao's books contain a wealth of circumstantial detail, all of which is paradoxically put into service of a view which denies value or reality to it. But McCutchion's basic point is still challenging. He implies that Raja Rao is terribly subversive in using the novel, which seems designed to convey "realism," to deny the ultimate reality of the phenomenal world. McCutchion points to two main features of *The Serpent and the Rope* which defy the conventions of the novel: first, "There is very little story":

> Of the more than four hundred pages, few are narrative, most are meditation – an unhurrying philosophical soliloquy on the nature of reality.

This observation is equally true of *Chessmaster* if not more so. Out of the 700 odd pages, only a few help to advance the story. Second, the novel defies conventions of space and time, so necessary in the "ordinary" construction of reality. Hence, "distinctions and identities are blurred":

> Rama is a Vedantin. Wherever he may be – in Madras, Aix-en-Provence, Pau, or Bangalore – his thoughts are outside space and time.

Again this is characteristic of Sivarama Sastri, the protagonist of *Chessmaster*, as it is of Rama. Hence, McCutchion argues:

> Since all is subjective illusion, there is no fixed reality upon which to build a novel, only a flux of impressions and interpretations.

This too might be said with equal justice about *Chessmaster*. McCutchion also observes that "too much solemn theorising on the infinite can be a bore," the sort of point that the Indian reviewers of *Chessmaster* seem to have made.

McCutchion locates the problematic of the book in its self-definition: how do we judge this novel? On its own terms or by the standards used to judge other novels?

> On its own terms Rao's book is hardly open to criticism: it is too long and repetitive . . . it is self indulgent, and undiscriminating . . . there is no development, it moves to no conclusion, ends where it begins. . . . The major fault of the book is its philosophical garrulousness.

But towards the end of his essay, McCutchion suggests a way of dealing with the novel on its own terms, by exposing what he sees as "The contradiction at the heart of Rao's novel":

> Rama tries to *live* in the world and *think* out of it. This gives rise to a kind of duplicity tearing the reader and hero between double standards – desire for happiness and justice in this world, coupled with lack of responsibility and decision because this world is not ultimately real.

Thus it is McCutchion who first suggests a way of reading Raja Rao "against the grain," a method later taken up with much greater methodological exactness by Paul Sharrad in *Raja Rao and Cultural Tradition* (New Delhi: Sterling, 1987).

To sum up, the crux of McCutchion's criticism seems to be his problem with Raja Rao's subversion of the form of the Western novel:

> The question might arise: is this a novel at all? . . . All the central concerns of the western novel are absent – social relations, psychological motivation, characterization, judgement, a passion for the concrete.

Today, we would not be so worried on the score. It has become customary to suggest that the form of the non-Western novel is quite different from that of a Western novel. Also that such novels often defy all the conventions and devices of the Western novel. They are thus the repositories of alternate world views, of different realities. The notion of time, space, causality, individuality, and reality itself are as culture bound as are conventions of narrative.[4] But in the process of offering what might appear to be easily discussable criticism of *The Serpent and the Rope*, McCutchion raises several crucial philosophical and interpretative problems that are suggested by Raja Rao's work. I shall refer to these later.

At this juncture, I had invoked McCutchion in order to make the point that all of his observations are as, if not more, true of *Chessmaster* as they are of *The Serpent and the Rope*. When I say that perhaps they are "more true," I am merely trying to underscore the feeling that Raja Rao seems to have gone too far this time. While the earlier novel was praised and hailed as a classic, *The Chessmaster* seems to have been viewed as an embarrassment. Even faithful Raja Rao fans do not seem to have wanted him to go so far. It would seem that even subversion of the Western novel, after all, has its limits. Raja Rao seems to have delivered an impossible sort of book, a novel that is really an anti-novel, a novel to end novels, a book that not only challenges, but actually resists reading in the normal sense of the word. In short, a book that makes impossible demands on its readers, strains their patience, and almost forces them to reject it.

I want to end this section with a review of my own experience of reading this book, so as to contrast it with the previous views. I think such an impressionistic recap has its uses, especially when attitudes to the book are still fluid and its interpretation has not yet become institutionalized.

The first reading was difficult. Until page 210, when Raja Rao introduces the theme of zero vs infinity, the former representing India and the latter the West, I found nothing really to hold on to. Siva's cerebrations seemed interminable and somewhat pointless. Like many of the other reviewers, I felt that I was back in the world of *The Serpent and the Rope*; the novel seemed to continue Rama's story, or was at least a more elaborate retelling of it. It was, at the same time, exciting to be back in Raja Rao's Paris. After page 210, the going was a little easier, until the last section of the book containing the much anticipated dialogue between the Brahmin and the Rabbi. This last section, I thought, was terribly tedious again. I kept marvelling at how nothing really happened in the novel. Even at the end the book is incomplete. We don't know what happens to Siva and Jayalakshmi or Siva and Suzanne. We don't know if Uma is finally cured of her sterility. Perhaps, all this is left for the next two parts of the trilogy. Overall, I thought that *Chessmaster* was a slower, sadder book—much more ponderous and opaque than *The Serpent and the Rope*. What was most curious was that though the central characters were all in their thirties, they seemed so *old*, really aged and ancient, as if they had the knowledge in their bones that they were playing out their karmic chessgame the millionth time; hence the depth of the weariness, of their *dukkha*, of their quiet, terrible, and deathly longing for liberation, *moksha*, or in the terms of the novel, for *sunya*, the zero, dissolution.

On rereading the novel, I found myself adjusting better to its pace. It demanded a different, unhurried, but concentrated attention span. This was not a book meant to be read by professionals, but by those with a deeper involvement in its central concerns. I was struck by its similarities with that other great text of Indian English poetry—*Savitri*. Like *Savitri, Chessmaster* is a very ambitious book, which aims at expressing a totality. Raja Rao wants to subsume and encapsulate an encyclopedic understanding of the world as we know it today in this book. Like *Savitri*, I thought, this is a book that a lot of people will resist and ignore, but which can't be dismissed. Its very presence—so huge and solid—means that it cannot be brushed aside and rejected. Certainly, not with the ease with which some of the reviewers have done so. The central issue is not so much its "literary merit," because carping about a lack of plot, looseness of structure, or repetition, only exposes the limits of our own critical standards. Indeed, the book demands to be judged by its own standards, which most of the reviewers have failed to do. And even if the verdict is that "it doesn't work," such a verdict cannot be passed as facilely as Nandakumar and Naik have done.

To say, "I can't stand Raja Rao and all his philosophical humbug" is one thing; we are all entitled to our opinions and tastes. But to therefore dismiss his project as hypocritical or unsound is illogical and unfair. The critic must engage with Raja Rao on the author's own terms, even if he wishes to disagree with these terms; to show these terms to be self-contradictory, fallacious, or ambiguous is to begin a constructive (even in the deconstructive sense) engagement with the text. One thing I felt sure about after my rereading is: Raja Rao is certainly not a poseur or a humbug. His involvement in the world of *Chessmaster* is absolutely genuine. Why else would he re-cover and remap the same territory that he traversed in *The Serpent and the Rope*? If nothing else, I was sure that Raja Rao deserved to be taken very seriously indeed, certainly not to be rejected outright as some of the reviewers had done. *The Chessmaster* may not become a very popular novel, but it is certainly a major work. I hazard a prediction: as the years go by, we will see more and more criticism on this book and perhaps one day it will be recognized as an acknowledged classic, one of the great Indian novels of this century.

II

Before I offer the record of my own engagement with the text, I want to clarify that I do not intend to offer a systematic reading here.

That would be too ambitious for a paper of this sort. Instead, I would like to offer some broad guidelines or approaches to Raja Rao and *Chessmaster*. I think that these interpretative strategies should help open up the text to other readers.

Let me start with an essentializing question: "What is Raja Rao's ideological project?" In other words, what is it that he's trying to do in his novels? When we say that he is a philosophical novelist, what is he trying to philosophize? The answer to such questions can, by no means, be simple and unitary. But I would like to propose an approach. Raja Rao's novels can be read as an attempt to validate and mediate what might loosely be termed "Advaita" in the contemporary world. The implications of this statement itself are numerous and not unproblematic. Advaita or non-dualism is a particular philosophical school which acquired a sort of primacy in Indian philosophical inquiry. Raja Rao's use of tradition is, certainly, more eclectic. But at least in the *Chessmaster*, he aligns his protagonist on the side of a kind of monism. The two key terms in my statement, "Advaita" and "contemporary world," seem to be contradictory. The moot question is whether Advaita can serve a useful function in today's world? Can it, for instance, solve the very real problems of colonialism and underdevelopment? It is not as if Raja Rao is unaware of these issues. Obviously, to claim that the phenomenal world is an illusion and only the Self alone is real—after Sankara—is not quite sufficient. Advaita has to be mediated and reinterpreted in the light of contemporary experience. Its efficacy and if I may say so its superiority has to be logically established.

It is this that is Raja Rao's ambition. His project is to show the viability of a world view which has been more or less eclipsed even from contemporary India. The only way that Raja Rao can make this philosophy viable is via a sort of modified existentialism. Advaita penetrates to the core of the flux that is the daily life of his characters, Ramaswamy of *The Serpent and the Rope* and Sivarama Sastri of *Chessmaster*. These characters negotiate life in an Advaitic fashion, thus demonstrating its efficacy in the contemporary world. This is somewhat like negating life even while one is living it, denying the ultimate reality of oneself even as one lives and suffers.

In *Chessmaster*, we have a particular version of Advaita that has, as I see it, the following major sources. One is the philosophical practice of Sri Ramana Maharshi and the other is the *sunyavada* of the Buddhist philosopher, Nagarjuna. Allied to the former is, of course, the philosophy of Raja Rao's guru, Sri Atmananda, and behind the latter is, equally obviously, the Buddha. In *Chessmaster*, not the realization of self is sought as in the earlier works, but a *dissolution* of self. While Moorthy, through right action, illustrates Karma Yoga; Rama, Jnana Yoga or the path of knowledge; and Govindan Nair, a type of Bhakti Yoga, of complete self-surrender to the Divine, Sivarama Sastri represents the power of negative dialectics, the attempt not to achieve something, but to vaporize one's self into nothing. Here the familiar dichotomies between the male and the female, vowels and consonants, India and the West, the Brahmin and the Kshatriya, the sage and the saint, logic and devotion, truth and the world, all hinge on the opposition between zero and infinity. The judeo-christian tradition is shown to represent the quest for perfect society here on earth, while India is seen as denying the validity of the world itself. The way out, for Raja Rao, is not to improve things as the saint-soldier does, but to dissolve contradictions completely. For him, all numbers dissolve into zero as they emerge out of it. Infinity is merely cumulative, while zero is total negation that cuts the root of illusion. One can never become perfect in time, but attain perfection only by negating time.[5]

For Raja Rao, the world belongs to the woman, while man is merely the instrument for its dissolution – Siva the destroyer, who alone can undo the generative power of Prakriti. The woman finds release by complete self-surrender to the man, who really represents dissolution. This only Jayalakshmi can understand; Suzanne and Mireille, on the other hand, want to continue their separate existences. The only meaningful dialogue, for Raja Rao, is between the Brahmin (zero, dissolution, negation) and the Rabbi (infinity, completion, affirmation). The former is vertical, denying time; the latter is horizontal, finding fulfilment through time. It is such a framework that provides the skeleton of the plot of the novel. The first part, "The Turk and the Tiger Hunt," shows the incompatibility of Siva and Suzanne like that of Rama and Madeleine in the earlier novel; the second part is dominated by Siva's affair with Mireille; and the third with the dialogue with Michel, the

Jewish holocaust survivor. The steadfastness of the Siva-Jayalakshmi relationship and the impossibility of its consummation, and Siva's relationship with his step-sister, Uma, and her inability to bear a child – these two relationships provide the glue that keeps the novel together. Moreover, there are the usual digressions, stories within stories, letters, diary extracts, and long speculative internal monologues that characterize Raja Rao's narrative technique. A certain degree of novelty is offered in two or three characters whose role in the plot is minimal, but who are very important – Abd'l Krim, the exiled Algerian leader, and Ratilal the French, Jain diamond merchant. Raja Rao had said in an interview that the book is a tribute and acknowledgement of the great suffering of the Jews on behalf of humankind; this is elaborated at length in the story of Michel. But the suffering of Michel does not make the world any more real for Siva; his solution to the world's problems still lies in self-extinction – not suicide, but an undoing of the self.

To end this section, let me try to place *Chessmaster* in the larger scheme of Raja Rao's oeuvre. Let me do so by reducing each novel to a formula and then looking for an equation that puts these formulae together into a meaningful relationship. In short, by doing a Raja Rao on Raja Rao. I see *The Serpent and the Rope* as a text which illustrates the ultimate incapacity of the intellect to resolve the human problem; Rama's relationships fail to take him to the Absolute just as all his philosophical disquisitions, however impressive sounding to others, fail to secure for himself the spiritual success that he so badly seeks. In the end, he acknowledges that only a Guru can save him. This guru is the irrepressible Govindan Nair of *The Cat and Shakespeare* who shows Ramakrishna Pai the way of the kitten – complete self-surrender or *prapatti*. This is thus an affirmative book, a book which ends in success. *Chessmaster* is neither an admission of defeat nor an affirmation of successs; here we don't see either the failure or success of Advaita. *Chessmaster* is an ambiguous book in which neither zero nor infinity wins. It accommodates not just the Brahmin and the Rabbi, but the Jain and the revolutionary – though the violent ways of the latter are viewed unfavourably through Gandhian eyes. *Chessmaster* moves beyond these positions to a kind of indeterminacy. Siva, Raja Rao's spokesman, is no longer always right. Nor does he pretend to be in full control of his metaphysical project. There is always the more powerful presence of the Chessmaster behind the movements of the characters in the book. Of course, any notion of the personalized Chessmaster or prime mover is just another version of the God that Siva would deny as the quintessence of the horizontal. But this is one of the contradictions of the book.

III

I have provided above a broad and highly selective summary of my reading of the book. This will serve both as an invitation to the text and also as my apology for not engaging with it more directly. Below, I will try to make amends providing a few approaches for interpreting the text, which I consider useful.

First of all, it is useful to see the book, as the reviewers have pointed out, as a rewriting of *The Serpent and the Rope*. It is in the earlier novel that we can see the most convenient entry point to the central dialectic of *Chessmaster*. Rama tells Savithri:

> Zero makes all numbers, so zero begins everything. All numbers are possible when they are in and of zero. Similarly all philosophies are possible in and around Vedanta. But you can no more improve on Vedanta than improve on zero. The zero, you see, the *sunya*, is impersonal; whereas one, two, three and so on are all dualistic. (205)

Chessmaster picks up this opposition, between zero and infinity, the impersonal and the personal, the monistic and the dualistic:

> Either you accept the world, and build a human empire, accepting death and, therefore, the pyramids (whether you called it a mausoleum for Mao or for Tutankhamen), or you transcend the world and as such death itself, and find the Truth of Sankara's 'Sivoham, Sivoham.' (145)

Or as Siva puts it cryptically in his dialogue with Michel: "The quarrel of man is between zero and infinity, between Truth – and God." (670)

But what is important to realize is that the philosophical positions in *Chessmaster* are more clearly defined and more neatly expressed.

Not only are the thematic preoccupations similar, they are carried out by similar characters in both the novels. Hence we can propose the following schema:

The Serpent and the Rope →	*Chessmaster*
Ramaswamy	Sivarama Sastri
Madeleine	Suzanne
Savithri	Jayalakshmi
Savithri's husband, Pratap	Jaya's husband, Surrendar
Anand (Savitri's brother)	Raja Ashok
Saroja	Uma
Saroja's husband Subramanya Sastri	Uma's husband, Ramachandra Iyer
Catherine	Mireille
Lakshmi	Rati
Grandfather	Father
Tante Zoubie	Madame X
Georgias	Michel
Lezo	Jean Pierre

The arrow mark indicates that the latter character has evolved from the former; sometimes the resemblances are so pronounced as to make them almost identical, at the other end of the spectrum, as with Anand turning into Ashok, the former is merely a hint. In all cases, there is a strong relationship, either in the traits of the two that make up the set or in their functions in the narrative. Not just the central characters, but incidents, events, discussions, and locations, and even the quotations are common to both books. The resemblances are more than a sense of *deja vu* and it would require a detailed paper to discuss their implications. I only want to say that those who have read and enjoyed *The Serpent and the Rope* will find easier access to *Chessmaster*; they will also have an added dimension of recognition as they read the latter text.

The second introductory tool has to do with Raja Rao's method of reasoning in *Chessmaster*. Except for a hint in Girija Kumar's review, other readers have not been able to figure out whether or not there is a system to Sivarama Sastri's philosophical disquisitions. Is his erudition simply impressionistic bandinage or does he work from some logical principles? Often, readers seem to be baffled by the numerous discussions in the book which seem vaporous, incoherent, and directionless. I have tried to clarify some of the important preoccupations of Raja Rao above, but here I want to unravel his method of reasoning and philosophizing.

Some clues are provided by the text. Siva is shown to be a mathematician in the book, but he hardly does any mathematics. True, there are references to Poincare, Pascal, Einstein, and above all to Ramanujan, and his goddess Namakkal, and a sprinkling of mathematical terminology throughout the book, but the fact is that Siva spends most of his time discussing philosophy with lovers, friends, and acquaintances. Raja Rao would imply that he is a mathematician not because he does mathematics, but because he uses a mathematical method to do philosophy. Siva explains his method somewhat like this:

> The fact is, like in any mathematical equation, you make a series of statements, and you reduce one to the other, till you get one clear class. As I was telling Michel . . . the only equation that now remains and remains to be solved, is the hindu-hebraic one, the vertical or the horizontal, I repeat, the zero or the infinity, historylessness or chronicling: Krishna or Moses. (260)

This method is found in its early stage in *The Serpent and the Rope* where Rama, the historian, spends most of his time in the same kind of discussions that Siva indulges in. As Savithri says of Rama:

> he works with symbols and equations. History for him is a vast algebra, and he draws in unknowns from everywhere to explain it. (183)

Or as Rama says to himself:

> And thus I tried to formulate myself to myself. I like these equations about myself or others, or about ideas: I feed on them. (195)

Similarly, Siva tries to find the equation or formula of ideas:

> in mathematics when you have a certain method to the solution of a problem . . . you apply the same method to all sets of problems in the same series. Similarly, when you understand one fundamental principle in indian [sic] philosophy, you apply the same method of interpretation to every other problem in the same system, the same series. And I treat all indian mythology as a set of equations, and I apply my technique to it, and the results are astounding. (271)

Or to put it more pithily, this is Siva's "new doctrine of mathematics or philosophy" – "words are numbers and numbers words." (318)

I would characterize Siva's method as a kind of reduction. The Latin root of reduce is *reducere*, to lead back – *re* (back) + *ducere* (to lead), whose past participle is *ductus* (a leading, conducting), which gives us the modern word, "duct," hence "conduce" and "conduct." Among the meanings of "reduce," these apply to Raja Rao's method: "to put into a simpler or more concentrated form"; "to bring into a certain order; systematize"; and "to break up into constituent elements by analysis" (*Webster's New World Dictionary*). Raja Rao rightly calls his method "a doctrine" because we realize, when we read his books, that his method is far from "scientific" or "logical." This logic is all his own kind; everything must have "instantaneous meaning"; that is why Swanston, the Cambridge leftist intellectual tells Rama, "There are too many incomprehensible factors in your statement, sir" (*The Serpent and the Rope*, 182). Raja Rao's method of reduction is, therefore, more poetic than philosophical in the traditional sense of the word. The knowledge that this method produces, is not knowledge in the strict sense of the term; it is more like a totalized realization. It is by employing this type of personalized, intuitional reduction that Siva comes to the conclusion that India represents the quest for zero, the vertical, the ahistorical and the abhuman, while the Judeo-Christian, Chinese, and Communist civilizations represent quest for the infinite, the horizontal, the historical, the human. Moreover, it is by this system that each character comes to represent some sort of abstraction, a formula, and relationships become equations – to be solved and resolved.

The third interpretative strategy that I find useful is to read the book against the grain. A beginning in this direction was suggested, as I mentioned earlier, by David McCutchion. Recently, Paul Sharrad has based his reading of *The Serpent and the Rope* on this principle. He refuses to accept the authority of Raja Rao and the power it confers on his male protagonists. Whereas other critics have been merely angry with Raja Rao or with his heros for being poseurs, narcissists, or male chauvinists, Sharrad sees in these figures a tension between contradictory forces. He views the text as the battleground for these forces. Instead of seeing the book as a coherent whole and its characters as rounded personalities, Sharrad would like to see them as divided internally by the contradictions and tensions of the culture they try to portray:

> I shall be going on to argue that every culture is founded upon contradictions and tensions between constructed coherence (unity) and natural disorder (plurality). . . . Rao's recourse to tradition, especially in a culture as complex as that of India, casts him into contradiction and plurality despite his quest for some unified, stable base, so that in *The Serpent and the Rope* he is paradoxically most Indian not because he upholds some 'official' cultural standards, but because he dramatises the inherent conflicts of his own and of any other culture. (16)

Raja Rao is, thus, seen as being Indian not because of, but in spite of, himself. Sharrad's book is a portion of his Ph.D. dissertation, "Open Dialogue: Metropolitan-Provincial Tensions and the Quest for a Post-Colonial Culture in the Fiction of C.J. Koch, Raja Rao and Wilson Harris," at Flinders University of South Australia (1986). As such, the book contains a lot of dispensable background information and observations on both Raja Rao and his milieu. Moreover, Sharrad's interpretation is not based so much on changed notions of the nature of a text or of reading, but is grounded upon a certain view of post-colonial culture as a picture of conflict, not cohesion. He sees a homology between cultural conflict and textual conflict, between the contrary pulls of post-colonial India and of Rama. The conflict, again, is defined in terms of the commonplace tradition-modernity paradigm. Thus, Sharrad's method is a type of "vulgar" sociology of literature, which is both simplistic and unilinear in tracing the influence of culture on literature. Yet, it is a valuable beginning in a new direction. For nowhere in the criticism of Raja Rao do we find an analysis like the following:

> The fundamental lack of authenticity in Ramaswamy's 'autobiography' derives from his attempt to play the roles of both victim and hero, provincial and metropolitan. He claims the mutually exclusive privileges of both roles – proclaiming the risks he takes while seeking protection, presenting himself as lover while revealing his incapacity for love, allying himself with figures of action but taking a passive stance in the face of events that might challenge his responsibility. (68)

Sharrad has thus shifted the ground from the similar "literary" analysis of McCutchion to cultural and ideological grounds. Here, I think, lies a great unexplored potential for rereading Raja Rao.

I would like to end this introductory essay on *Chessmaster* with a beginning in this direction. The *Chessmaster*, as I see it, is the most powerful attempt in contemporary English literature to temporize and legitimize an ideology that denies the reality of the phenomenal world. In doing this Raja Rao is going against the dominant culture not only of the West where he has spent most of his life, but of today's India. This book defies the dominant culture not only in its content, but also in its form. It goes against the practices of the Western book trade with its cynical consumerism, cheap sales gimmicks, and corrupting system of incentives and threats. This is not the kind of book which will be promoted at black-tie cocktail parties or expensive publishers's bashes. This is an embarrassing book to have been written in the present world. Certainly, no "mainstream" author could have written such a book and found a publisher for it. It has no relevance to contemporary issues or to current publishing trends. It does not fit into any slot, not even into the slot of the great Indian English novel. It has not been written merely for the here and now, but for the hereafter.

Mulk Raj Anand once said to me about Raja Rao, "It's not enough to go on and on about Atman and Brahman, about the reality of Brahman and the illusion of the world; it won't do to cling blindly to Sankara's Advaita of the ninth century. Our problems are different.

How do we solve them? Can Sankara's answers serve us today?" These were challenging questions for an admirer of Raja Rao to answer, so I kept quiet. But on reading *Chessmaster*, I think I have found at least one way of answering them. Raja Rao does not deny the world or its suffering, brutality, and violence. His book is imbued with the very real problem of *dukkha*, the cosmic sorrow that Buddha sought to eliminate from the world. Raja Rao's book does turn a blind eye to history or its record of cruelty, to Birkenau and Buchenwald. He does not neglect politics, economics, or history. But to challenges that the human being faces anywhere – whether in Paris, London, or Calcutta – Raja Rao's answers point inward, from the exterior to the interior, from the outside to the inside, from the world to the self. Each one of us, he seems to say, must perform this little operation on ourselves – to dissolve ourselves into the nothing from which the whole world was created. To put an end to ourselves and thus to solve, once and for all, the problem of humanity. Deny yourself to become *That*. To me it is not this philosophy or its viability that are important, but the enormous energy and artistic integrity with which it is mediated through seven hundred pages of *The Chessmaster and His Moves*. However unreal the philosophy is, the characters are real, their suffering is real, their concern with the human problem is real.

However tempted we may be to do so, we cannot dismiss this book or ignore it. That would only be to deny and repress what we don't find palatable in our present understanding of literature and of the world. Our rejection will tell us more about ourselves than about the book, just as our acceptance of the book tells us more about our predispositions than about the virtues of the text. The problems are ours, not the book's.

NOTES

1. This information has been gleaned from a number of sources including Raja Rao himself, his publisher, Vision Books of Delhi, Professor Braj Kachru of the University of Illinois, and from the special *World Literature Today* number on Raja Rao (Autumn 1988). In an article in the latter, R. Parthasarathy identifies other

two parts of the trilogy as "The Daughter of the Mountain" and "A Myrobalan in the Palm of Your Hand." (561)

I would like to thank Mr. L.S. Ramaiah, Librarian, C.I.E.F.L., for lending me the special number of *WLT* on Raja Rao.

This essay was written in August 1989. Reviews or articles on the book which have appeared subsequently have not been discussed. For instance, the November 1989 issue of *Debonair* contained a review of the book by Gulshan Taneja which I have not discussed here.

2. I have, necessarily, to be vague about the identities of these critics because they know Raja Rao personally and would not like to be quoted. Of course, they know me personally too, which makes me more circumspect.

   Raja Rao himself seems not to be not displeased with the difficulty level of his book: "It is a *very* complex book. A lot of my friends said they found it impossible to read. R.K. Narayan said it went completely over his head." ("A Writer and his Moves" by Anuradha Chopra, *Times of India*, 29 October 1989, p. 8)

3. McCutchion's article appeared first in the Writers Workshop *Miscellany*, No. 8 (September-October 1961), pp. 91-99. It was reprinted in his *Indian Writing in English: Critical Essays* (Calcutta: Writers Workshop, 1969, pp. 69-82) and again in Meenakshi Mukherjee, ed. *Considerations* (New Delhi: Allied, 1975), pp. 90-101.

4. See, for instance, the essays by Viney Kirpal and Helen Tiffin in "A Symposium of New Approaches to the Criticism of Commonwealth Literature," *The Journal of Commonwealth Literature*, XXIII, 1 (1988), pp. 145-81. I have discussed this issue in my paper, "The Ideology of Form: Notes on the Third World Novel," to be published in *Social Scientist*.

5. For an excellent introduction to Indian philosophy see P.T. Raju, *The Philosophical Traditions of India* (London: George, Allen and Unwin, 1971). For a more detailed exposition see, Surendranath Dasgupta, *The History of Indian Philosophy*, 5 vols. (1922; rpt Delhi: Motilal Banarsidas, 1988). I have not attempted a detailed discussion of these sources here.

'The Sanskrit Charge' in Raja Rao: The Word and 'Sabda Tattva'

S. RAMASWAMY

He who possesses Sanskrit can possess himself.

Raja Rao, *The Serpent and the Rope*, p. 37

Anādi nidhanam brahmam sabdatattvam yadaksharam
Vivartate arthabhāven prakriyā jagato yatah.[1]

Bhartrihari, *Vakyapadiya*, Canto I, Sloka 1

[That beginning and endless One, the imperishable Brahman of which the essential nature is the Word . . . manifests itself into objects and from which is the creation of the Universe.][1]

I

In the Keynote Address given at the South Asian Languages Analysis Roundtable Conference at the University of Texas at Austin in 1984, Raja Rao spoke about "The Ultimate Word"[2] which takes into account the entire range of Sanskrit language and literature from the Rig Veda Samhita through the *Mandukyopanishad* to Sankaracharya on the one hand and to Bhartrihari and Abhinavagupta on the other. This is what the present writer would like to designate the 'Sanskrit charge.' This same 'Sanskrit charge' is evident in Raja Rao's 'metaphysical novel'— *The Serpent and the Rope*.[3] The point about the 'Sanskrit charge' is that it is carefully counterbalanced by what might be called the 'French charge' both in the Keynote Address and in the novel. In the address, there are fairly extensive quotations from Louis Renou, Paul Valery, George Poulet and Mallarme as there are quotations from Charles Baudelaire, Villon, Valery, Ronsard, Hugo and others in the novel. Briefly, the present writer would like to confine himself to the 'Sanskrit charge' and argue that the theoretical basis for discussing the 'Sanskrit charge' in Raja Rao's novels like *The Serpent and the Rope* and *Comrade Kirillov* is found in the Keynote Address given at the SALA Conference in 1984. The 'sphota' theory spoken about in Bhartrihari's *Vakyapadiya* was the quintessential point of reference in an earlier essay by Raja Rao entitled "The Writer and the Word,"[4] and the discussion of the 'sphota' and the 'sabdatattva' form the core of Raja Rao's novel *Comrade Kirillov*.[5] In both "The Writer and the Word" and "The Ultimate Word," the focus of interest is the word 'mantra' and the two novels in question provide an objective correlative for the conceptual enactment of Raja Rao's theory of the 'Word'. It is worthwhile relating this theory of the word as 'mantra' to Sri Aurobindo's "Poetic Vision and the Mantra.[6] The scope of the present paper, however, is extremely limited. Here the present writer would like to argue that there is an intimate connection between the essays of Raja Rao on the 'Word' and his novels. Indeed, his novels are an experiment – a successful experiment – in 'Word play' with a difference – a play or 'leela' with the 'Ultimate Word' – the realization of 'Sabda Brahman'.

II

Though the concept of the supreme word-principle 'Sabdabrahman' is found in Sanskrit texts right from the Veda downwards, the first complete postulation was perhaps given by Bhartrihari in his *Vakyapadiya*. Let us start with working definitions of the 'Sphota' as given by Bhartrihari:

> Sphotarupavibhagen dhvane grahanamishyate
> Kaischid dhvani sanvaidhya swatantro-anyaiah prakalpita.
> [Certain theorists maintain that reception of the sound takes place without any separation of it from the form of the Word

(sphota); others hold that the sound is not perceptible. According to yet others it is an independent manifesting agent].[7]

The definition of 'Sphota' and 'Dhvani' by another school:

> Yah sanyogvibhagashyam karanairupjanyate
> Sa sphotah sabdajāh sabdā dhvanyo aniah rudrahritah.
> [The sphota is that which is produced by the union and disunion of the speech organs (like the vocal chords). And dhvanis are sounds born of this sphota.][8]

As Subramania Iyer puts it: "Whatever be the form of the Sphota – sentence, word or phoneme – Bhartrihari mentions all the three – it is manifested by the sounds. The process of manifestation is described elaborately in the *Vakyapadiya*, with the help of as many as fifteen analogies, each illustrating one aspect of the doctrine.[9] Indeed, Raja Rao refers to this edition in his "The Ultimate Word." He gives his own rendering of the purport of the first Sloka of *Vakyapadiya*. Raja Rao has said:

> "The Brahman," says the *Vakyapadiya*, "the Brahman who is without beginning or end, whose very essence is the Word (sabda) who is the cause of the manifested phonemes, who appears as the objects from whom the creation of the world (seems to) proceed. Brahman is called phoneme (akshara) because it is the cause of the phoneme." Thus begins *Vakyapadiya*, the celebrated text on: The Phrase and the Word. And Bhartrihari, its great author continues:
> Idam ādyam padasthānam sidhi sōpanaparvanām
> Iyam sā mokshamananam ajihma rājapaddatih.
> [This is the first step in the ladder leading to salvation: this is the first royal road for all those who desire liberation.][10]

Of the various analogies used in the *Vakyapadiya*, only two will be glanced at here:

> Nādsya kramjanyatvān purvau na parashcha sah
> Akramah kramrupen bhedvaniv jāyate.

[The Word is neither a 'previous' nor a 'subsequent', because it is the speech-sounds which are produced in sequence. But the non-sequential is revealed as if it were divided.][11]

This is described in the form of an analogy in the next stanza:

Pratibimbam yathanyatra sthitam toye kriyavashat
Tatpravritimivān veti sa dharmah sphotanādyoh.
[Just as a reflection found elsewhere (i.e. in the water) appears, due to the activities of the water, to partake of the movements of the water, similar is the relationship between Word and speech sound.][12]

The other interesting analogy which very effectively illustrates the relationship between the Word and the speech-sounds is this:

Dvarpādānasabdesu sabdau sabdavido viduh
Eko nimitam sabdānāmparoarthai prayujyate.
[Grammarians consider that there are two 'word entities' (elements) in functional words; one (the sphota) is the cause of (the production of) words and the other (the speech-sound) is used in connection with meanings.][13]

This again, is beautifully illustrated through an appropriate analogy in the stanza:

Aranistham yathā jyotih prakasantarkārnam
Tat sabdoapi budhisthah jhutinām karnam prithak.
[Just as the light which is in the fire-stick acts as the cause of further lights, similarly, the Word which is in the mind is the cause of speech-sounds.][14]

The beauty of the 'Sanskrit charge' is that even difficult grammatical and technical thoughts are conveyed through 'upamana', the third 'pramana' (coming after 'Pratyaksha' and 'Anumana') so that it can be easily comprehended and remembered. Raja Rao, talking about this relationship between the Word and the speech-sounds, in his essay "The Writer and the Word" says:

> Is the word 'Rama' then eternal? the combination of 'Ra' with 'ma' which makes the word 'Rama', you will remember, creates a new entity. 'Ra' and 'ma' together is not 'Ra' plus 'ma' but is in fact beyond both sounds, hence it becomes a word. And so, when you can pronounce the word correctly, and say 'Rama', you create a vibration which, when it dies in the hearer (we have not yet come to the reader) you have another person who experiences the sound at the end of which experience he should know Rama in the way in which you wanted Rama understood. So that Rama must mean the same thing to you and to him and as such Rama has to be of an unchanging nature. Thus a vibration or a series of vibrations must mean at all times the same thing, for otherwise you would not have used it, and the hearer would not understand it as such. This comes to mean finally that he who says the word communicates the word and he who hears it has to have the eternal part awakened in him so that there could be right communication. If the transient speaks to the transient it becomes cacophony. But if the eternal, the unchanging, speaks to the unchanging we have one language. (p. 2)

Raja Rao refers to Bhartrihari and the 'sphotavada' not only in his essays on the Word but also in his novels. The following passage from *Comrade Kirillov* makes this abundantly clear:

> "The word consists of many atomic components – called Sphota" – he explained.
>
> Hence this Sphota accepted by all as the central word principle shining in the heart. It only manifests itself to us when expression is desired, as the sound which has received the impress of the positions and efforts (ordinarily employed in sound productions). . . .
>
> The word principle is conceived as having four stages, Para, Pashyanti, Madhyama and Vaikhari. The first is beyond comprehension; the second is attainable only by yogis; the third Madhyama is the Sukshma only to one's innate powers of hearing; the fourth is the word as we have it in use. Now it is the third among these that is accepted as the Sphota above enunciated.

> The word reduced to its sound value, then to its vibratory value, then finally to its etheric (*Akashic* is the Sanskrit word for it) structural value, is reduced to exact nothingness. It is this universal nothingness that makes all permutations possible. In modern language, we would say all objects are ultimately reducible to the electromagnetic field and sound and object being one, they can be interpreted in terms of the wave equivalents, etc.
>
> . . . A set of human, vocal vibrations – and in this case teleprinted probably – only produce the required physico-chemical transformation of the auditive and cerebral mechanisms, and produce a recognisable sound effect. Then the word is born.[15]

Subramaniya Iyer, in his study of *The Vakyapadiya*, comments on this phenomenon described by Raja Rao in his novel. Iyer explains:

> Even though each sound causes the cognition of the whole sphota which is thus its object, it has the form of the sound with all its properties such as accent, duration, timbre and so on. Whenever a cognition has one thing as its object and the form of another, it is an error. When we mistake a rope for a snake in the dark, the rope is the object of our error but the error has the form of a snake. The rope is the object because, after all, it is the rope which is in contact with the senses and not the snake. Similarly, the sphota is the object of cognition of each sound but it appears as the sound. In other words, when we finally get a clear cognition of the sphota, it is through a series of errors that we come to it . . . it is through a series of errors consisting in cognising the sphota in the form of sounds that we finally grasp it in the form of sphota itself.[16]

This explanation of the 'sabda-tattva', the relationship between the sphota and the Word is extremely relevant for the discussion of the Word in Raja Rao's writing as it even uses the same well-known analogy of the serpent and the rope to symbolize the difference between Appearance and Reality as is the case in the celebrated novel of Raja Rao, *The Serpent and the Rope*. Indeed, one should see here in purely linguistic terms the novel as the perfect 'objective correlative' in Eliotian terminology. The 'sphota' is 'the rope' and the words that are used and the situations that are conjured up amount to 'the serpent' in the novel. In fact, there is a direct reference to Bhartrihari in the novel:

> Father was a mathematician, and when he was not able to solve a problem, he would turn to Sanskrit grammar. Panini was his hobby all his life, and later he included Bhartrihari among the great Grammarians.[17]

In the interests of brevity, only this one reference to the text of *The Serpent and the Rope* should suffice here.

III

To sum up the argument. In his Keynote Address to the SALA entitled "The Ultimate Word," Raja Rao has said:

> Every movement I make is 'samskara', ritual, every statement I make, the sanctifying word, 'mantra'.[18]

In his own novel already referred to, *Comrade Kirillov*, he makes a reference to 'the sanctifying word, mantra':

> "I was thinking of the value of the word," continued P . . . "I have studied the Mantra-sastra a bit in my own day. Do you know what Mantra-sastra is? It is the science of the holy word – of the creative syllable . . . " he talked at length on this Indian theory of the Word.[19]

According to Sri Aurobindo, 'mantra' represents the highest intensity of the revelatory word. He explains:

> This intensity belongs to no particular style, depends on no conceivable formula of diction. It may be the height of the decorative imaged style as often we find it in Kalidasa or Shakespeare; it may be that height of bare and direct expression where language seems to be sued as a scarcely felt vaulting-board for a leap into the infinite; it may be the packed intensity of language which uses either the bare or the imaged form at will, but fills every word with

> its utmost possible rhythmic and thought suggestion. But in itself it depends on none of these things; it is not a style, but poetic style itself, the Word; it creates and carries with it its elements rather than is created by them. Whatever its outward forms, it is always the one fit style for the Mantra.[20]

What is argued here is that Raja Rao is an 'upasaka' of the 'mantra' – as a successful experimenter with the 'holy word', with 'the creative syllable', using the 'packed intensity of the language' as a 'vaulting-board for a leap into the infinite – to the attainment of 'Para-Vak' and this 'Para-Vak' is the 'Ultimate Word'. As Raja Rao himself has put it:

> Unless the author becomes an UPASAKA and enjoys himself in himself (which is Rasa) the eternality of the Word (Sabda) will not manifest itself.[21]

This is 'Sabda Tattva'. The Word indeed is eternal. To put it in the words of Bhartrihari:

> Nityave kritaktve va tesāmādin vidyate
> Praninămiv să chaisă vyavasthā nityatochayte.
> [Like living beings, words also have no (traceable) beginning whether they are eternal or created. This rule (about words) is called their eternality.][22]

In both his essays, "The Writer and the Word" and "The Ultimate Word," Raja Rao speaks of the 'Para-Vak' which is the 'Sabda-tattva'. For example, in "The Writer and the Word," he says:

> "Unless the Word becomes mantra no writer is a writer and no reader is a reader" and talks about giving "sound back to silence" and the "seemingly divided" remaining "undivided" and quotes "Mauna Vyakhya prakatita parabrahma tattvam."[23]

In his "The Ultimate Word," Raja Rao, speaks of the 'Para-Vak' as the

> Ultimate Word, the silence beyond silence, the origin and the end of the phoneme. Therefore is poetics (or grammatology) a way to salvation (moksha).[24]

We began with Bhartrihari. Let him have the last word as well:

> Tasmādyah sabdasanskarah sā sidhih parmātmanah
> Tasya pravrittitattvagyast udabrahmāmritamisyate.
> [Therefore, attainment of faultless speech is the attainment of Brahman. He who knows the secret of its functioning enjoys the immortal Brahman.][25]

NOTES

1. *Bhartrihari, The Vakyapadiya*, Cantos I and II with English trans. by K. Raghavan Pillai (Motilal Banarasidass, Delhi, Patna, Varanasi, 1971).
2. Raja Rao, "The Ultimate Word," Keynote Address to SALA, 1984. I am grateful to Sri Raja Rao for not merely giving me a copy of this but for also encouraging me to explore the concept of 'the Word' in Sanskrit.
3. Raja Rao, *The Serpent and the Rope* (John Murray, London, 1960).
4. Raja Rao, "The Writer and the Word," originally published in *The Literary Criterion*, Vol. VII, No. 1, Winter 1965. Reprinted in *Critical Essays on Indian Writing in English*, ed. M.K. Naik, S.K. Desai, G.S. Amur (Macmillan, Silver Jubilee Student Edition, 1977). The page numbers refer to this edition.
5. Raja Rao, *Comrade Kirillov* (Orient Paperbacks, 1976).
6. Sri Aurobindo, "Poetic Vision and the Mantra" in *The Future Poetry* (Sri Aurobindo Ashram, Pondicherry, 1972) pp. 29-37.
7. *The Vakyapadiya,* Sloka 81, p. 18.
8. *Ibid*., Sloka 102, pp. 22-23.
9. *Bhartrihari: A Study of the Vakyapadiya in the Light of Ancient Commentaries,* K.A. Subramaniya Iyer (Poona, 1969), p. 161.
10. Raja Rao, "The Ultimate Word," p. 3.
11. *Vakyapadiya,* Sloka 48, p. 10.
12. *Ibid*., Sloka 49, p. 10.
13. *Ibid*., Sloka 44, p. 9.
14. *Ibid*., Sloka 46, p. 10.
15. *Comrade Kirillov,* pp. 95, 96-98.
16. Subramaniya Iyer on *Vakyapadiya,* p. 163.

17. Raja Rao, *The Serpent and the Rope*, p. 18.
18. Raja Rao, "The Ultimate Word," p. 1.
19. Raja Rao, *Comrade Kirillov*, p. 95.
20. Sri Aurobindo, *The Future Poetry*, p. 28.
21. Raja Rao, "The Writer and the Word," pp. 2-3.
22. *Vakyapadiya*, Sloka 28, pp. 5-6.
23. Raja Rao, "The Writer and the Word," p. 2.
24. Raja Rao, "The Ultimate Word," p. 7.
25. *Vakyapadiya*, Sloka 132, p. 30.

Survival of the Narrator's Voice: An Introduction to the Telugu Novel *Ekaveera*

P. RAMACHANDRAIAH

It is more than fifty years since Raja Rao, speaking about the Indian novelist's task of expressing the "tempo of Indian life," told us:

> There must be something in the sun of India that makes us rush and tumble and run on. And our paths are paths interminable.[1]

But one wonders how many of these "paths interminable" have found critical acceptance in this half-a-century. For our critical procedures have always tended to block off many an appealing literary performance because the constitution and bylaws of the novel framed by a Percy Lubbock, a Ford Madox Ford or a Warren Beach keep a suspicious vigil over our responses to such a performance. And, to how many people would it not have sounded like a sacrilege of their sacred sense of modernity when Raja Rao, in the same breath, reminds us – of all things – of the ways of the Puranas where "episode follows episode, and, when our thoughts stop, our breath stops"?[2]

Readers of Indo-English fiction know that, in the comments mentioned above, Raja Rao's focus is on the force of the breathless speech which suggests the presence of the narrator in the oral narrative modes of the ancient times, such as the Puranic. In times when reading materials were not easy of access and when the written word was rarely resorted to, the teller or singer of a tale presented his narrative discourse orally to an audience or to another narrator – like Suta to Saunaka, Agni to Vasishta, Parasara to Maitreya, Visampayana to Janamejaya, or Vyasa to Ganesa. When, after the spread of the written word, such narratives came to take the form of written compositions, the speaking voice of the narrator persisted in them, with myths, legends, episode and moral and philosophical reflections forming part of the discursive strategy. This is because writing, as Walter Ong has told us, "can never dispense with orality,"[3] and this is more true of cultures such as those of India or West Africa. Never fully divorced from the literary tradition, the oral tradition steals into every poem, short story, or novel in these cultures where "reading a text means converting it into sound."[4] Though this tradition might have yielded to the growing power of the written word in many literatures of the world, mercifully this process does not seem to be complete in Telugu literature. That is why, till recently, both poets and common readers in Telugu spoke only of 'telling a poem', 'making a poem', or 'weaving a poem', and only rarely of 'writing a poem'.

One of the commonplaces of Indo-English literary criticism is that it is an intelligent use of the oral mode of the puranas that gives a special force to Raja Rao's narrative art. We would perhaps become more sharply aware of this force, if we go beyond genre-prescriptions, and, as Robert Scholes and Robert Kellogg have advised us, beyond the tendency "to view the novel as the final product of an ameliorative evolution."[5] And I believe that there is many an Indian narrative work which can be fruitfully related to the line of *Kanthapura*. My attempt here is to examine, in this light, the Telugu novel *Ekaveera* written by the Jnanapeeth-awardee, Viswanatha Satyanarayana.

Let me begin by taking note of Satyanarayana's mode of composition: he always dictated his narrative and non-narrative works to a scribe. Fortunately for us, this great writer was not unduly influenced by the British Victorian novel which had already rendered the Telugu reader's view of narrative literature "almost hopelessly novel-centred,"[6] by being the readily-available model for any practitioner of fiction at that time. For, without being dismissive about the well-made novel produced by this model, we may say that it came to have a limiting influence on the imaginative skills of the Telugu novelists who made a religion of this model, regarding it as an inexhaustible source to be blindly drawn upon at all times. Willing to be more tightly caught up than their western counterparts, in the post-Jamesian dogmas of impersonal narration, these imitative novelists perceived the genre as a rigidly prescriptive one which cannot transcend components like an omniscient or first-person narration, a linear progression of the story, a realistic presentation of events and people, and a partial or (preferably) complete disappearance of the author from the scene so that the story 'tells itself'.

I believe that one of Satyanarayana's claims to uniqueness – though this uniqueness sometimes tends to slip into idiosyncracy – rests on his refusal to conform to the available model. It is the inability of a great mind to fit into a mould which cannot meet the demands of his transcending genius. That is why some of his novels like *Haha hoohoo* and *Veyipadagalu*, besides *Ekaveera*, are far removed from what we may call the mainstream Telugu novel, often inviting complaints about their alleged deficiency in realism, episodic structure, authorial presence and use of myths, and above all about their being no novels at all! Which explains how caged the critic has been in the written word, or in the concept of narrative discourse as a construct of only written words, apart from his inability to respond when a writer attempts to bend a genre to his needs.

A prominent example of such an attempt is *Ekaveera*, a historical novel set in the times of the Nayaka Kings of Madurai. It is a story of thwarted love, in which the young prince Kuttan and his friend Veerabhupathi are, by a quirk of fate, each married to the woman in love with the other. The tensions and tempests involved in such a love-quadrangle, however, fail to provoke the victims to clash with the social norm. Here, a 'realistic' novelist would have found a naturalistic presentation irresistible, or plumped for the lachrymose sentimentality of a Guinevere-Lancelot type of situation. In such a familiar fictional dialectic, either Ekaveera or Meenakshi would yield to the 'stormy sisterhood' of Charlotte Bronte, our extra tears would be won for the erring, passionate victim, and finally a Racinian kind of psychological realist would take over from the narrator. But such thematic cliches are not for Satyanarayana who would be the director of – not a panderer to – the readers's sensibility. That is why he makes the story assert the traditional matrimonial ethic, and charges the story with the strength of the oral tradition of the puranas, though he does not present a first-person narration.

We are given a foretaste of this kind of narration in the very beginning of the book when the narrator tells us, in what sounds like an 'unnovelistic' way, that "there is a story about the wedding of Lord Sundareswara and Meenakshi," and then digresses briefly into the myth of Lord Siva's creation of the river Vaigai. This digression is something more than a mere rhetorical strategy: The all-consuming hunger or thirst of the demon Kundodara here serves as a parallel to the flames of passion which consume the four chief characters in the story. And the river Vaigai, which is said to have been released by Lord Siva to quench the thirst of Kundodara (who, though demonic, is nevertheless a follower of Siva), becomes a metaphor for Kuttan, later in the narrative, to assert the indivertibility of the course of his love. Is such a love, then, sinful or sacred? If there is an ambivalence here, what are its implications for the moral purport of a puranic narrative which this 'novel' is? These questions which involve a delicate manipulation of the responses of the 'recipients of the narration' call for the continued presence of the guiding, moralizing narrator in the narrative.

And the narrator, in his turn, establishes his presence, with a torrential narration which is hard for the western reader to contend with. Throughout, the presence of a listener or audience is suggested by the narrator's explanatory comments which would perhaps sound incongruous in what has come to be crowned as the 'showing' method. Some of these comments are about what happens around the Vaigai river in different seasons of the year, about the royal custom of having one's body wiped by servants after bath, about the educational, political and military affairs of the Madurai Kingdom, and its architectural excellence, about the greatness of Saint Avvayyar, about the navigational skills of the ancient Andhras and about the dacoit menace around the 'Pandyakammai' tank in those days. The narrative speed is marked by the readiness of the narrator to meet his listeners half-way, depending upon their needs and capabilities, such as when he reminds them of 'the times of the story' or of the 'things mentioned in the earlier part of the narrative.' At one point, in the moral or philosophical tone of the puranic narrator, he allows himself a digressive aside about what he calls the exhibitionist tendencies of women with regard to their jewels or wealth. Especially, when he says that the readers and Kuttan should forgive him for divulging Kuttan's love-secrets, the narrative act becomes a sort of collaborative endeavour in which the readers are called upon to participate. To object to this, or to judge it according to the dictates of the nineteenth-century realism, is to be unable to identify with the readers of the early puranic times who could accept the narrator not only as the story's moral or social commentator, but also as one of the characters, like Vyasa in the *Mahabharata*. A sensitive imaginative adjustment to the various postures and roles assumed by the narrator is a prerequisite for responding to any story in the oral tradition.

But the structure of *Ekaveera* is not episodic, like those of the puranic narratives in which the various illustrative 'upakhyanas' (discourses within the discourse), or the long philosophical reflections, are not always sought to be linked with one another or with the central motif. In spite of the longish discourses such as those about the origins of kuchipudi dance or about the proselytizing activities of the Portuguese priests, the book has only a seeming episodicality which conceals a skilful interweaving of different strands of experience, a gradual build-up of the structure of the events, in which the recurring metaphor of river is made to reflect the changing moods and situations of the lovers.

Therefore, Satyanarayana's aim here is not a point-to-point imitation of the puranic mode; and his choice of it is not prompted by an inept craftsman's love of the freedom offered by its flexible form. This can be seen in character-portrayal also. The puranic mode often leads to a kind of 'externality', because the narrator positions himself between the audience and the character and comments on the outward gestures and utterances of the character, unlike in the novel form whose rhetorical devices make for the conception of a character from what Eliot calls 'some emotional unity'. Still, Satyanarayana succeeds in making the characters – especially those of the lovers – come across clearly and in presenting their conflicts with a measure of psychological realism – though he does not intend his book to be a psychological novel.

But, this is not to deny that the narration falters occasionally. To me, the account of the defeat of the Portuguese priest in his debate with Ekaveera seems a little palpable, awkwardly standing apart from the story-line. Besides, the narrative goals of this book cannot equal those of *Kanthapura* in which the old-granny-narrator's habit of mixing tenses is cleverly used as a stylistic device to suggest a merging of the past with the present, a sense of the continuum of life, which is so typical of the puranic narrator's cyclical concept of time. Nevertheless, in the stereotype-ridden world of Telugu fiction, *Ekaveera* could be regarded as an effort to widen the bounds of the novel. In terms of the experience it communicates, the book turns out to be much greater than its parts when related to the oral tradition.

NOTES

1. Foreword to *Kanthapura* (Oxford, 1974), p. vi.
2. *Ibid.*
3. *Orality and Literacy: The Technologizing of the Word* (Metheun, 1982), p. 8.
4. *Ibid.*
5. *The Nature of Narrative* (OUP, 1966), p. 1.
6. *Ibid.*, p. 8.
7. *Selected Essays* (Faber and Faber, 1932), p. 212.

Gandhi and the West

C.D. NARASIMHAIAH

What one great man owes to another is something really difficult to assess and it is futile to seek to determine the extent of any such influence except when curiosity prompts one to trace the origin of an idea or attitude. It is no sign of maturity in a people to care for it too much, for ultimately ideas themselves matter less than what use they are put to. Throughout her long history India has always been encountering other peoples drawn to her shores by love of her wealth or learning—possibly one of the reasons why Indian culture has a continuity, not in a static, but vital, way. She came in contact with the Egyptians, the Greeks, the Chinese, the Arabs, the Central Asians and the peoples of the Mediterranean, and during the past three hundred years, the Europeans. Only the Europeans stayed apart while the others intermingled with us. Precisely because of this encounter of contrasting cultures there has been some unrest but it has also sustained and stimulated Indian life. In any case the encounter hasn't produced a 'mastizo culture' that sprang up, say, in the countries of South America which imitated Europe in ignorance of their own cultures. Much less has the encounter encouraged India to devour other cultures and destroy their identities, as the monolithic American culture has done, apparently in its praise of unity of culture. A composite culture has been India's pride through the ages. And this is an acute insight of Gandhi's considering how little, one feared, Gandhi had known of the American scene.

It is curious but perhaps true that while Tagore the internationalist wrote in despair that the English-educated Indian's voice became an echo, his whole life a quotation—he did not feel the impact but was a servile receiver, Gandhi seemed at first to have greater faith for all his apparent horror of Western civilization. He believed that if the mass of English-educated Indian youth are not entirely denationalized it is because their ancient culture is too deeply rooted in them – the reason why the leaders of the Indian Renaissance in the nineteenth century, while they admired English education and English institutions, their total response was by and large from a strong Indian base; indeed, they responded to these on their own terms. Two of the most outstanding examples are Raja Rammohan Roy and Vivekananda.

For a descendant of these, Gandhi must have, to start with at least, looked quite disappointing. He was just past twenty when he went to England weathering "formidable opposition" from his own relations. Why did he go? "In a word, ambition!" he said later. But it was not vague, it had a purpose, it was his "cherished goal" to become a barrister, but also to see England "the land of philosophers and poets, the very centre of civilization." It was a callow young Indian that affected the "English gentleman," wore frock coat and top hat, and took lessons in music and dancing. He learnt to take care of his consonants and cultivated the habit of deliberate articulation. This as well as his early meticulousness in dress persisted to the end of his life whether in the way he used words (the way he resisted "smart expression" and "cultivated" words "carefully and prayerfully" or in the manner he wore his loincloth and let the elegant folds of his shawl sit on his shoulders. The "English gentleman" was only destined to be the "springboard" from which to take a leap forward, but first of all to repudiate what he so much sought after. For very soon, almost everything Western came under fire, samples of which are contained in expressions such as these: "Satanic civilization" of the West; "the glamour of the West," "the Golden Fleece," "to run after (which) is to court certain death"; "Europe today is only nominally Christian. In reality it is worshipping Mammon"; insatiable material ambition at one end, and consequent war at the other"; "our geography is different, our history is different, our ways of living are different . . . where there are millions and millions of units of idle labour it is no use thinking of labour-saving devices." And the consequent "boycott" and burning of "British goods." As with economy so with the art of government – he reacted sharply against "parliamentary democracy." He, an oriental, with standing accusation against the East by the practitioners of allopathic medicine of indulging in occultism, had the courage to hit back on Western medicine as "black magic" which demoralizes man with its "palliatives" instead of "strengthening his character."

From innocent, thoughtless imitation to almost unqualified condemnation! But there were bridges between. After his return from the Round Table Conference, he refuted the irreconcilable doctrine of the East and the West and proclaimed to his countrymen: "I have been convinced more than ever that human nature is much the same no matter under what clime it flourishes and that if you approached people with trust and affection you would have ten-fold trust and thousand-fold affection returned to you." Not a particularly well-phrased sentiment but even a banality, because it is Gandhi, does reflect his faith in the irreducible minimum of good that is in all men. He resiled from extreme positions and evinced positive interest in wanting to "profit from the light that came from the West" – "light" "not glamour." He will not bar his doors and windows against the West. "Let all the cultures," he said in an oft-quoted remark, "of all the lands blow about my house, but I shall refuse to be swept off my feet by any." And from this position of tolerance, he can move on to firm faith in the West: "Let us engrave on our hearts the motto of a Western philosopher: plain living and high thinking" – again, a trite remark for the aesthetically-disposed but such was Gandhi's terrific earnestness that the cliché did not inhibit his full response to the ideals that were held up before him. I must hasten to add that Gandhi has not progressed chronologically from one position to another, in the way I have enumerated; I have only tried to classify for convenience some of the significant shifts in his complex reaction to the West and I shall have occasion to dwell in detail on his more complex responses to the West presently.

Dr. Oldfield in his book *My Friend Gandhi* speaks of two kinds of Indians that came to England: some that fail in their encounters with a different mode of life and these "commonplace minds" "drop into the ordinary run of English diet, English habits and general mediocrity. And the other can stand firm in their faith and be prepared to die for it and they prove themselves men indeed." He adds: "Upon this class of men does the mantle of Gandhi still fall and the future of India depend."

It is well known that Gandhi's vegetarian obsessions in England brought him in contact with some of the finest Englishmen of the day, some of them well-known Socialists and ardent Christians. One of them commended the Bible to Gandhi's attention with "Read the Bible if only for my sake." The Old Testament sent him "to sleep" but he had a profound experience when he came to the New Testament: "My young mind tried to unify the teaching of the *Gita, The Light of Asia* and *The Sermon on the Mount*. That renunciation was the highest form of religion appealed to me greatly." "But I say unto you, that ye resist not evil" and "if any man take away thy coat let him have thy cloak" delighted me beyond measure. "It was the New Testament which really awakened me to the rightness and value of Passive Resistance." But this great admirer of *The Sermon on the Mount* "refused to set Jesus on a solitary throne" – words which echo Vivekananda's ruthless critical analysis of Christianity in his American speeches.

Pyarelal, in his very fine piece of writing on Gandhi, remarks: "Socialism in England came under two kinds of leadership – under pioneers like Henry Salt and Edward Carpenter it hoped that Labour would return to the land and become simple in its needs. But the Webbs, Shaw and Hyndman representing the other shade of thought preferred an industrial community. The former lost the day." Perhaps true.

But Pyarelal likes to believe, and that is what disturbs one, that Gandhi "picked up the last thread and applied it to the uplift of the Indian villages." According to him, these, namely, vegetarianism and handicrafts became "the two central planks in India's non-violent struggle for independence under his lead." This, I fear, is a very misleading impression, as both ahimsa (which in any case is very different from the cult of vegetarianism as practised in the West) and handicrafts have had several thousand years of history in India. All one can say is that even the approximation and sophisticated articulation of these very old Indian practices by British intellectuals may have pleasantly surprised Gandhi who apparently had originally associated England with mechanization and meat-eating. In any case the British or even Irish intellectuals could not have brought much conviction either into their own thinking or, to one like Gandhi on vegetarianism, as we can see from Bernard Shaw's remarks: It is as mean to send the cow to the slaughter-house when she becomes old as to send your mother to the gallows when she falls sick or has ceased to give suck. A typically (clever) Shavian statement!

Well, the strongest word Shaw uses is "mean." One hadn't thought that to send a mother to the gallows was just a "mean" act (unless the word is diluted of its meaning) but Shaw's desire for effect must have outrun his sense of precision for words. Besides, Shaw's objection is presumably to sending an "old cow" to the slaughter house. This celebrated vegetarian wouldn't probably have had any objection to the killing of a fat calf or a milking cow. Now compare with this Gandhi's reference to the cow as a "poem of pity"; that it is a symbol of the entire sub-human world; and to respect this "gentle animal" is for man to be "taken beyond his species and to realize his identity with all that lives."

It is the same with Socialism and handicrafts for which Gandhi is said to be indebted to Ruskin. Let us leave Gandhi for a while and try to understand the Western writers who find themselves in juxtaposition with Gandhi because of his own acknowledged indebtedness. There are whole papers devoted to each of them and I am only trying to comment in passing on the degree of relevance in associating Gandhi with these writers. It is embarrassing to trace influences, enumerate parallels and cite cross-references in the manner of school boys. For what is far more rewarding is to understand how each of these great men including Gandhi is a product of his milieu, to know the challenges his environment posed and assess his response as an expression of a complex of his tradition, his milieu, his personal temperament and his unique vision of life. The object of this paper is to try and offer some sort of concerted, informed corrective to glib generalizations about influences on the basis of superficial resemblances and expressions of indebtedness made in modesty; in any case, to gain a critical appreciation of what Gandhi did with the ideas he took from others, in comparison with what the Western writers themselves did with their own ideas.

Consider Ruskin, to start with. Towards the end of the eighteenth-century, England witnessed unprecedented industrial development and all those ills which Dickens describes in moving terms in a succession of novels – insanitary slums, starvation wages and drunkenness of the poor. Ruskin traces all the ills to the pillage of the labourer: the landlord pillages the peasant, the lawyer pillages the client and the merchant everyone by adulterating foodstuffs. We are told that women and children in mines pulled large wheelless tubs laden with coal. And then, he saw "a wilderness of spinning wheels," yet the people had no clothes; "every leaf of English greenwood" was blackened with coal, and yet the people died of cold; harbours were full of ships laden with wheat, but the people died of hunger.

Eminent thinkers like Malthus wrote: "To prevent recurrence of misery is alas! beyond the power of man," and *The London Times*, we are told, endorsed it and explained it away as the result of "Nature's simplest laws." Even so sensitive an intellectual as John Stuart Mill maintained that political economy had nothing to do with moral judgments. And William Morris, disciple of Ruskin, was convinced that only by violent usurpation of power could the masses free themselves from their masters. How perilously close to the "dictatorship of the proletariat"!

Now, briefly, this was the background against which Ruskin had to operate. Fortunately for him the air was charged with reform: George Eliot preached the Religion of Humanity in novel after novel; and Carlyle preached the Gospel of work – he asked if all the financiers of Europe could undertake in one joint-stock company to make one shoeblack happy beyond an hour or two, for the shoeblack has a soul other than his stomach. Ruskin who admired Carlyle enormously joined in with his Gospel of social justice. Thanks to the religious background at home, provided largely by his mother, and his study of Plato, Ruskin's "rage against inequality became divine." Like Gandhi, Ruskin too put the emphasis on the personal character of the reformer. "Here I am," said Ruskin trying to reform the world, "and I suppose I ought to begin with myself." One reads of instances in his life, of street-cleaning, road-digging, sinking an enormous fortune in lands and houses for philanthropic purposes, and volunteering services in the Working Men's College. But primarily "to fill starved people's bellies is the only thing a man can do in this generation," he asserted again and again.

He knew he could not expect the higher classes to initiate reform. Parliament, to him, was "darkness voluble"; it was a "circumlocution office." And neither ballots nor barricades, he believed, would alter man's condition and so he tried to touch their hearts through the ethics of Christ. His artistic predisposition lent strong support to it. As an artist he believed that mindless mechanical perfection is not good for man – it produces a new class of slaves, mindless tools rather than man. The artist who believed in the whole man, in the totality of experience and not in its fragmentariness, opposed the division of labour as the division of man – "learning to make points of pins and heads of nails." He pleaded that "England feed all hungry, not merely the deserving hungry, nor the industrial hungry nor the well-intentioned hungry." Instead of organizing a labour movement, he advocated "filial loyalty from the employee and fatherly benevolence from the captains of industry." One is constrained to add that this paternalism did not work – "the labourer's voice was worth a rat's squeak" – it didn't work any more than Gandhi's trusteeship theory did, though the latter met with considerable success in Gandhi's own life-time and at the hands of his disciple Vinoba Bhave. But what interests readers of Ruskin nearly a century after is the way he "mobilized" sentiment by "every telling biblical phrase, every word that had overtones of feeling" to win attention to his views. He was among the first of modern thinkers who brought emotion into what Carlyle called that "dismal science" of economics and "morals into the law of supply and demand." Where a Gandhi would innocently repeat the biblical statement, "Man does not live by bread alone," Ruskin the artist would add, "but also by the desert manna, by every wondrous word and unknowable work of God." It is by such felicity of phrasing, religious fervour, and sincerity of purpose that Ruskin could exert the kind of influence he did: "in no other socialist movement has Christian thought had such a powerful leavening effect," wrote Mr. Clement Attlee, the Labour Prime Minister. And one gathers, too, that Ruskin's *Unto This Last* was a potent influence with a considerable number of Labour Members of Parliament in England.

But that was not immediately – it was more than half a century after Ruskin's death. St. George's Guild which Ruskin founded was in a quandary in Ruskin's own life-time. Those "perplexed souls" of the Guild never quite knew what their master wanted. For while they were seeking help in co-operative farming, we are told that their master was purchasing emeralds for the Guild Museum at Sheffield or was off in

Venice making studies of "Dream of St. Ursula." He offered grandiose plans to control the flooding of the Rhine, the Rhone and the Po and liked others to emulate his example all along the Alps. "If *they* don't do," all Ruskin could do was to say, "it is their fault – not mine." He said very bravely, though: "But if I die, I will die digging like Faust" – this was mere attitudinizing when one recalls the earnestness with which Faust and, equally his creator, Goethe, addressed themselves to social welfare. Now, what could the men do with what a critic of Ruskin calls their "dreary, dilatory, make-shift master who preferred painting flowers to reforming the world?" It is true that the master couldn't help his insanity. He had at least the sense to wind up the affairs of the Guild at once – "so that I may come out of it with clean hands and a pure heart." It is obvious he was not meant to start a movement. There is pathos in the way he described himself as "a reed shaken with the wind." And for others, what remains is fortunately not so much his own example but his exhortation, the impact which the exhortation of a writer has on his readers for generations to come:

> Raise the veil boldly; face the light and if, as yet, the light of the eye can only be through tears, and the light of the body through sack cloth, go thou forth weeping, bearing precious seed, until the time comes.

The time came, not for Ruskin but to one who read him, literally to go about with a sack cloth. A friend of Gandhi put into his hands a copy of Ruskin's *Unto This Last* to read during his journey from Johannesburg to Durban: "The book was impossible to lay aside, once I had begun it," says Gandhi. "It gripped me. Johannesburg to Durban was a twenty-four hours' journey. The train reached there in the evening. I could not get any sleep that night. I determined to change my life in accordance with the ideals of the book." Not determination only, but he "arose with the dawn ready" "to reduce these principles into practice." The result was the Phoenix Settlement, an impossible ideal, "the beautiful vapourings of an unpractical idealist," rendered into a most practical proposition, "the blueprint" for his reformistic work. Comparison of St. George's Guild with the Phoenix Settlement is superfluous for those who are acquainted with the origin and working of both. Suffice to say that for Gandhi, social obligations had a profound religious sanction as the evocative expression *Daridranarayana* connotes – the reason why he could declare with conviction that even God dare not appear before a hungry man except in the form of food. He was not content to talk about spinning and working with hands but did it all himself and lived on the most frugal diet, and the barest minimum of clothing possible. To those who preached the Western brand of Socialism in India, Gandhi would say in the characteristic Indian way that he admired their concern and sacrifice but since he could not keep pace with them he would ask them to stop for him in their march, collect him, and take him along with them, which meant respect for the individual. He feared that Communism was a natural corollary to the Socialism of the West, and he did "not want to rise on the ashes of the blind, the deaf, and the dumb." In their Socialism, these will probably have no place. "I want freedom for the full expression of personality. I must be free to build a staircase to Sirius, if I want to." For Gandhi, socialism will not wait till "all were converted" but "starts with the first convert." He illuminates his stand with a vivid image from mathematics: "If there is one such you can add zeros to the one and the first zero will account for ten. . . . If however the beginner is a zero . . . multiplicity of zeros will also produce zero value." One now appreciates the unusual importance Gandhi attaches to purity of conduct in a leader. He said his socialism is "as pure as crystal . . . requires crystal like means to achieve it." To him socialism was a religious creed, not a political ideology.

The comparison of Gandhi with the writers of the West is all to Gandhi's advantage when we come to Tolstoy. Born a Count, Tolstoy inherited a huge property of several estates covering more than five thousand acres with more than three hundred serfs and their families. His own father's retirement from government service on ideological grounds and the misrule of successive governments especially the bureaucratic regime of Nicholas I fostered in Tolstoy a mistrust of government. Add to it the rise of the self-seeking and corrupt, capitalistic bourgeoisie who were a "parasitic drain" on the peasants. His social conscience was stirred by the contrast between the "godly" life of the peasants and the egotistic life of his own class. He began to renounce pleasures and live for others.

Tolstoy realized that only three types of life are possible: the egoistic, the social and the Christian. "The history and the destiny of humanity" consisted for Tolstoy in passing from the egoistic to the Christian attitude – surprising how so great a man could only think within the Christian framework while talking of the history and destiny of man as though Christianity was all the religion that mankind professed or practised. That is by the way, but is interesting how, in contrast to Tolstoy, Gandhi was far more inclusive – he included every religion in his scheme of things and studied everyone of them assiduously. "I do not believe in the exclusive divinity of the Vedas. I believe the Bible, the Koran and the Zend Avesta to be as divinely inspired as the Vedas." Tolstoy too, like Gandhi, disapproved of the egoistic life totally; but unlike Gandhi, Tolstoy thought, the social was vague: "humanity is fiction and it is impossible to love it." And it followed therefore that only the last one was man's destiny. Following this Tolstoy insisted on two things; the dissolution of the armed forces; and the ownership of the land by the peasantry. No wonder Lenin recommended in 1910 the widest publicity for Tolstoy's work as an aid to the socialist revolution.

But the revolution that ensued was not the one that Tolstoy worked for. He ruled out violence of all kinds whether of the Church or the State – the violence of the Church has gone, we know, but what of violence of the State? Tolstoy was up against a Church which existed in the name of Christ, but its connivance at violence, he held, "perverts the teaching of Christ." This perversion of truth by the Church and the exploitation of the peasantry by the State became an obsession with Tolstoy. In his *Kingdom of God is within You*, he compiles evidence from Europe, America and Russia to show how everyone subscribed to Christ's teaching of "Resist not evil." In Russia itself, he pointed out how some peasants refused to take up military service on religious conviction. They submitted readily to the most cruel punishments but refused to render military service. Tolstoy comments: They were sent to Georgia and the Commander-in-Chief of the army was asked to "correct them." That was the end of their non-resistance. The argument against Tolstoy's non-resistance is that Christ's teaching is not in harmony with our industrial age; if so, Tolstoy would say, "do away with machines." He saw that mechanization threatened to substitute "the pulsing of the machine for the rhythm of nature."

His view of art after conversion to Christ's teaching must be understood in this context. He pleaded: Art must remove violence, only art can do it; and only that art which unites people in the same feelings and promotes brotherhood among men is great art—the reason why he rated Dickens higher than Shakespeare. Gandhi was to denounce the Taj Mahal on the same ground—to him it was no work of art, but an embodiment of slave labour. He would, one supposes, have approved of the temples of India and the cathedrals of Europe as works of art because they were built out of the prayers of pilgrims. We know he did prefer the music of the spinning wheel to everything else except perhaps that of the *Gita* and the *Ramayana* of Tulsidas, by the same criterion as Tolstoy's. Now, come back to Tolstoy. A year before his death Tolstoy spoke—yes, it was all speaking or writing—passionately at the Peace Congress of 1909 in Sweden and asked the Congress to make their choice: "We have to repudiate either Christ and his teachings or the State with its armies and war." His countrymen have kept both, paid lip-service to one and actively fostered the other· teaching good, oh, unteachably after evil! The point I am at pains to make is, Tolstoy renounced all he had, himself lived nobly and simply but could not be the leader of the revolution, —*that* was reserved for Lenin. Tolstoy's work ended with protests, passionate speeches, and addresses to peace conferences. Now Gandhi reads Tolstoy's *The Kingdom of God is within You* when, in his own words, he is passing through a severe crisis of scepticism and doubt. He explains its impact on him: "I was at that time a believer in violence. Its reading cured me of my scepticism and made me a firm believer in non-violence. What has appealed to me most in Tolstoy's life is he practised what he preached and reckoned no cost too great in his pursuit of truth!" What, one asks, was the cost Tolstoy paid for pursuing truth? Renunciation of luxuries in his own life and living a life of truth? But what is that compared to the cost of making non-violence the creed of millions involving all of whom in an encounter with a "satanic" government? Within ten years after the commencement of his struggle for independence in India, and three decades before his death, a colonial of the most powerful empire on earth had the courage to say at a public meeting organized by

Students of the Benares University in 1920, when there was not a ray of hope for India's independence:

> All of us have had many anxious moments while the Viceroy was going through the streets of Benares. There were detectives stationed in many places. We were horrified. We asked ourselves: "Why this distrust. Is it not better that even Lord Hardinge should die than live a living death?" We may fret, we may resent but let us not forget that India of today in her impatience has produced an army of anarchists. I myself am an anarchist, but of another type.

Now where did Gandhi get this courage from? Not from Thoreau or Tolstoy though they may have given him support for what was within him. It came mainly from the deep wells of Hinduism:

> If we trust and fear God, we shall have to fear no one, not Maharajas, not Viceroys, not detectives, not even King George. I honour the anarchist for his love of country. I honour him for his bravery in being willing to die for his country.

The West had heard the language of military strength of the despot and the conqueror, and of assertion of the mob against the tyrant but it had not heard the voice of warning from the man of God after the Renaissance. Note some of the expressions Gandhi used at the time: "Such an empire cannot live if there is a just God ruling the universe." He knew "he was playing with fire," but he had the gumption to tell the Imperial government on another occasion that if he was set free from prison he "would still do the same." Now he spells out the future course: we have "now reached almost the end of our resources in speechmaking, and it is not enough that our ears are feasted, that our eyes are feasted, but it is necessary that our hearts have got to be touched and . . . our hands and feet have got to be moved."

Every word drips with energy and it is a call to action, for non-violence is truly the weapon of the brave man who cannot shy away from action in the name of thought; only in the context in which he found himself in India, then action meant for him "the quiet courage of dying without killing." As Jawaharlal Nehru writes in his *Discovery of India*:

> A bitter sense of humiliation and passionate anger filled our people. All the unending talk of constitutional reform and indianization of the services was mockery and an insult when the manhood of our country was being crushed and the inexorable and continuous process of exploitation was deepening our poverty and sapping our vitality. W had become a derelict nation.

And there is the refrain of helplessness in paragraph after paragraph of Nehru's writing: "Yet what could we do, how change this vicious process?" or "How could we pull India out of this quagmire of poverty and defeatism which sucked her in?" It was when the country was in this "quagmire" of despondency that Gandhi came. In Nehru's words, again, for hardly anyone has realized so acutely and critically the significance of Gandhi's emergence on the Indian scene as Nehru has done:

> And then Gandhi came. He was like a powerful current of fresh air that made us stretch ourselves and take deep breath, like a beam of light that pierced the darkness and removed the scales from our eyes, like a whirlwind that upsets many things but most of all the working of people's minds. He did not descend from the top; he seemed to emerge from the millions of India, speaking their language and incessantly drawing attention to them and their appalling condition. . . . Get off the backs of these peasants and workers, he told us, all you who live by their exploitation; get rid of the system that produces this poverty and misery. Political freedom took new shape then and acquired new content.

Now can we say this of any of the three writers from whom Gandhi has drawn stimulus for his work: that he did not descend from the top; that he seemed to emerge from the millions of India, speaking their language. Well, precisely, this is the measure of Gandhi's success, as it is the measure of *their* failure in one sense. Only Thoreau, of all the three writers, seems to come closest to Gandhi though from his own account, what he borrowed from Thoreau is only a name, for Satyagraha has been in practice in this country for centuries and Gandhi himself had practised it in South Africa, both when he was thrown out of the first-class railway compartment and when he was beaten in the streets after his arrival there – and both these happened much before he had ever heard of Thoreau's "Civil Disobedience." Gandhi writes: "My first introduction to Thoreau was, I think, in 1907 when I was in the thick of the passive resistance struggle. His essay on Civil Disobedience left a deep impression upon me. I translated a portion for the readers of the *Indian Opinion*, which I was then editing. The essay seemed so truthful and convincing that I felt the need of knowing more about Thoreau and I have read his life, his *Walden*, and his shorter essays with great pleasure and equal profit."

But Thoreau, alone, of the three writers, lived in many respects in a manner Gandhi would have most approved of – I have in mind the objective and the urgency with which Thoreau went to live in Walden, preached the abolition of slavery, rallied to John Brown's aid, and himself refused to pay the toll-tax because the money went to a wrong cause – waging of the Mexican war – and for refusing to pay the tax, went to prison, though only for a day. Only he, among the three writers of the West, may be considered to have lived the most virtuous life; only he showed himself capable of some action. And his passionate desire for action comes out again and again in statements like:

> There are nine hundred and ninety nine patrons of virtue to every virtuous man.
>
> There are orators, politicians, eloquent men by the thousand but the speaker has not yet opened his mouth . . . who is capable of settling the much-vexed questions of the day.
>
> Man must :eason from the hands and feet to the head, not the other way.

Everyone of these Gandhi would have endorsed most unhesitatingly.

There are, besides these, many minor but important resemblances in the modes of living of Thoreau and Gandhi and precisely because of their close resemblance, I think it is most fruitful to take a close look at the life and work of Thoreau and Gandhi, more so because Thoreau was the only one of the three who had made a reasonably close study of the Hindu books most of which had also influenced Gandhi so profoundly. He often compared himself with the Hindus, bathed in the pond early morning considering it as sacred as the Ganges's water, ate rice, kept away from meat and drink, read the *Gita*; and felt so ecstatic that he thought one line from the *Gita* was worth the whole state of Massachusetts put together; and in comparison with its wisdom "our Shakespeare" was "green" merely.

He did not escape into the Walden forest but went there to transact some private business – to front the essential facts of life, to drive life to a corner and suck the marrow out of it, to see what it is like to live according to the dictates of one's conscience and then proclaim the results to the world instead of going there in the evening of one's life. Besides he has many lives to live and cannot give too much time to any one. And then, for him, to live is to live a life of simplicity, independence, magnanimity, and trust. Consider the terrific urgency and impatience with which question follows question to get at the truth of life: "Why do men degenerate ever? What makes families run out? What is the nature of the luxury which enervates and destroys nations? Are we sure there is none of it in our own lives?"

It was evident to him that the mass of mankind live "mean and sneaking lives," "lives of quiet desperation." Thoreau's question was: is it necessary? Well, he must try it out himself, the way Gandhi made his experiments with Truth. Being a writer Thoreau could well have said with Keats: Axioms of philosophy are not axioms until they are tested on our pulses. For he did test it all. It is an experiment which lasted two years two months and two days. It is interesting that he left Concord for Walden on 4th July when the rest of the country was in jubilation, even as Gandhi was in riot-torn Bengal on the day of India's Independence, rather than in New Delhi. Only, Thoreau was in solitude while Gandhi was in the thick of work. And these two essential attitudes are to me very important in the understanding of these two men. Thoreau was sick of the incessant activity and insatiable wants of his countrymen – the labours of Hercules are nothing before them, he says, because they are only twelve while those of mankind have no end. Why do people work for six days in the week forged in their "own golden or silver fetters" and keep the seventh day for Sabbath, instead of the other way: work for one day – it was enough to work for one day – and keep the other six days for the joy and wonder of creation. For all his love of Shakespeare and the values he represented Thoreau had the audacity to write:

Tell Shakespeare to attend some leisure hour
For now I've business with this drop of dew.

For he thought you will not find health in society, but in nature. "Society is always diseased, and the best is most so." Stevenson is reported to have remarked humorously that "Admetus (whose flock Thoreau grazed) never got less work out of any servant since the world began." But Thoreau's defence was: what need is there to "keep farms, houses, barns, cattle, and farming tools" all "more easily acquired than got rid of." He claimed that he himself kept no dog, cat (and what is more interesting in our comparison of Thoreau and Gandhi), cow or spinning wheel. Except for the cow and the spinning wheel, especially the latter, Gandhi himself might have said all that Thoreau did say, but it is in the manner in which experience came and the way the organization of experience showed itself in the corresponding organization of words that the distinction between the two should interest not merely students of literature but those who seek to judge Thoreau and Gandhi – judge them by what they *thought* or *said*. And ultimately except for the generation that knew Gandhi first-hand, the world, including his own countrymen, will have nothing to go by but their writings and recorded speeches.* And so judged, how do they emerge? Consider a few examples of what they said and the responses they evoke in us. Take such simple things as food, clothing and shelter to which Gandhi made repeated references. Gandhi abstained from meat-eating, and much of what he said or did in this regard simply had a long and hallowed religious sanction and there simply was no questioning it. As for Thoreau, he was "not unusually squeamish." "I could," he says, "sometimes eat a fried rat with a good relish, if it were necessary." And he had his support in the 'Ved' from which he quotes: "he who has true faith in the Omnipresent Supreme Being may eat all that exists" and is careful to qualify it with: "Vedant limits this privilege to the time of distress." But he gave up flesh because it was not "agreeable to my

* It is interesting, however, that the Buddha is judged by the mass of mankind, not by his teachings but by his life, his great example and it is as such that he has entered the mainstream of Indian thought and legend. Gandhi believed primarily in action and in support argued that "the rose does not need to write a book or deliver a sermon on the scent it sheds." That is how he himself became an intimate part of the Indian legend. Where he sat became a temple and where he trod the ground was hallowed, Nehru was to say in Gandhi's own life-time. And Gandhi had to fight against the Mahatmahood himself.

imagination" and anyone who cares to preserve his "poetic faculties" must "abstain from animal food," for even nations are "betrayed" by their "vast abdomens," "such apparently slight cause destroyed Greece and Rome, and may destroy England and America." Lastly, it is his compassion for all that is living that argues against killing animals: "Who hears the fishes cry?" or "The hare in its extremity cries like a child." The "remarkably adult yet innocent expression of their (partridges') open and serene eyes is very memorable. All intelligence seems reflected in them. . . . Such an eye was not born when the bird was, but is coeval with the sky it reflects. The woods do not yield another such age." When man has his passions under control and is pure, it marks his "flowering" and he "flows at once to God when the channel of purity is open." It is by placing things in their larger perspective that he invests even the commonplace with a significance – the illumination comes from multiple sources.

This is how he presents – the presentation is an enactment – the necessity for clothes. Clothes, he says, must be a necessity, must be the result of a "crisis in our lives." He seeks support for his stand analogically: "The loon retires to solitary ponds to spend it. Thus also the snake casts its slough, and the caterpillar its wormy coat by an internal industry and expansion." A real compulsion from inside, not vulgar fashion must make way for new clothes. But what is the world's way? He says: "The head-monkey at Paris puts on a traveller's cap, and all the monkeys in America do the same. That is why dressing hasn't risen to the dignity of an art." His sense of humour, though grim, was extraordinary. One remembers what Gandhi said: But for my sense of humour I should have committed suicide.

Now move on to Thoreau: As for clothes, so for shelter. His plea is for spending more time in the open than indoors. Consider how he marshalls arguments in his favour: Children do, poets and philosophers do; so do the peasants. Above all, Thoreau sees in it a cosmic reason: there shouldn't be "obstruction between us and the celestial bodies"; then he clinches his point with an illustration from the ways of birds: "Birds do not sing in caves nor doves cherish innocence in dovecots."

From commonplace observation, he moves on to human civilization for an argument: "If civilization is a real advance in the condition of man it must be shown that it has produced better dwellings without making them more costly." And there is his own personal example: didn't he build his house single-handed and complete it according to the needs of the seasons? It cost him only \$ $28.12\frac{1}{2}$ – the way he kept strict accounts! Only Gandhi could surpass him – no other writer, not Ruskin, not Tolstoy in this respect – as is revealed from the scrupulous accounting of every pie spent by him in London as a student and later as a public servant in South Africa and India.

Thoreau has recourse to classical mythology to reinforce his point about cheap dwellings: "Momus objected to the house which Minerva made because she had not made it movable, by which means a bad neighbour might be avoided." Yet another example, this time from history, Egyptian history: "The myriads who built the pyramids to be tombs of the Pharaohs were fed on garlic, and may be, were not decently buried themselves." Thoreau would rather have their bodies drowned in Nile or thrown to the dogs than be buried in pyramids. And one more example from humdrum life, now to rouse the conscience of civilized man: "The mason who finishes the cornice of the palace returns at night perchance to a hut not so good as a wig wan." And so "It certainly is fair to look at that class by whose labour the works which distinguish this generation are accomplished." It is not enough to say that there must *not* be palaces for the few and huts for the millions; the case has to be worked out. If it is not worked out, as it was not by Gandhi, is that the price the man of action, always pushed around, pays for not nourishing his imagination? But do imagination's mercies accomplish what perpetual nagging may fail to do? Howsoever trivial is the example Thoreau cites, see how he can raise it to a higher place because of the profound truth only *felt experience* can convey: he had, it seems, three pieces of limestone on his desk and he was terrified to find that "they required to be dusted daily when the furniture of my mind was all undusted still, and I threw them out of the window in disgust." An act like this and the pressure behind the words can do more than all the sermons against acquisition of things. He seized upon significant things and actions in the life of man and dramatized them as only an imaginative writer can do, for example, the way he conceived the fewness of things! He said he had only three chairs in his house: one for solitude, two for friendship and three for society. This is not a matter of scholarship only (for Gandhi claimed he could have written

Marx better if only he could summon to his aid scholarship) but of imaginative apprehension of the truths of life in commonplace things, when things become images and images in turn assume the status of symbols. Truth seldom dawns on us as effectively as through a symbol. It must therefore he admitted that whatever Gandhi thought of Marx, he could not have presented the case for simple living with the compulsion of a Thoreau, the compulsion being the gift of art. For, despite his protests to the contrary,

> My life has been the one I would have writ
> But I could not both live and utter it,

he did succeed in both, though, in the one, only in a limited way, but certainly in a remarkable way compared to writers like Nathaniel Hawthorne whose grievance against the Brookfarm experiment was: "you cannot idealize manual labour." Besides, Thoreau's justification for not undertaking mass reform was: It is not important that all should be as good as you but there "must be some absolute good somewhere to leaven the lump," as was evident when Gorky remarked on seeing Tolstoy sitting on a boulder near the sea "I am not an orphan on this earth so long as this man is alive"; the same has been said for Thoreau: "There can be little doubt that the spirit of *Walden* has pervaded the American consciousness, stiffened the American lip, steadied the American nerve, in *ponderable degree*."

Like Gandhi, Thoreau too was opposed to the technological civilization, but how memorable his reactions have become whether it is against the railroad, or the post and telegraph. It is his unusual ability to bring things into focus and perceive clearly that makes for memorableness. Consider some of these: "We do not ride the railroad, it rides upon us"; or, why do you lay telegraphic wires across continents? is it to get the first news that Princess Adelaide has whooping cough? As for letters, he doesn't remember receiving or writing more than one or two letters of any worth in all his life.

But artist that he is, there is freedom from fads and consequently one sees an ambivalence in his attitude. There are times when he can get excited by "the poetry of the railroad," how it brought life to the wilderness or how the railway whistle has electrified the atmosphere and is glad to note that "to do things the railroad fashion is now the word." In the same way the hum of mere telegraphic wire was "aeolian harp" to him and sent him back to Greek poetry. He would distinguish between simplicity as a fad and simplicity born of wisdom, and in support of the latter he would argue, "It is not the tub that makes Diogenes, the Jove-born, but Diogenes the tub." It is here that some of Gandhi's fads inhibited emotional response and simplified thinking. His ear, for example, was so attuned to the music of the spinning wheel that its hum, it seems, drowned every other music; rather, it filtered out all music but that of the spinning wheel (and, of course, that of the *Gita* and the *Ramayana*). He showed very poor understanding of poetry when he wrote to Tagore that the "poet sings for the morrow," and asked him in passionate language to leave his Muse and spin on the *charka*. For "India is a house on fire: let the poet bring his bucket of water." And this is the penalty a reformer pays for his passion for reform – it seems to block the channels of sensation and perception, except the few that the reformer wishes to keep open.

Now Thoreau did not claim to reform the world exactly, though he was vexed by the "tragedy of mediocrity." He declared: "The only obligation which I have the right to assume is to do at any time what I think right." What sounds anarchical is somewhat softened by a plea for tolerance for the otherness, as we see in the following: "If a man does not keep pace with his companions, perhaps it is because he hears a different drummer. Let him keep pace to the music he hears." But in the process he is so lost in responding to the drumbeat of his own choice that he begins to believe in the rightness of his own actions and develops self-esteem bordering on narcissism: "The greater part of what my neighbours call good I believe in my soul to be bad, and if I repent of anything it is very likely to be my good behaviour. What demon possessed me that I behaved so well." Now this is clearly not merely self-esteem but bad taste born of a supreme sense of one's own infallibility.

But one has sympathy for Thoreau when he takes the position: Your fellowman to whom you are apprenticed is "ever bolting right the other way"; and so it is futile to waste your time in trying to go along with him. "The man who goes alone can start to-day . . . (not) wait till that other is ready." Besides, "you are not drilling soldiers, who may turn out hirelings after all." When provoked he would go so far as to say "I came into this world, not chiefly to make this a good place to live in but to live in it, be it good or bad"; and as for himself, he would "rather keep a bachelor's hall in hell than go to board in heaven." It is clear that he eschews social obligations from his sphere of obligations – his obligation is primarily to himself, not in a narrow sense, but to the higher law that governs his life; he must go where his genius leads him. In following the call of his own genius he is not ashamed of reconciling himself to the theory of the survival of the fittest:

> I am not responsible for the successful working of the machinery of society. I am not the son of an engineer. I perceive that when an acron and a chestnut fall side by side, the one does not remain inert to make way for the other, but both obey their own laws, and spring and grow and flourish as best they can, till one, perchance, overshadows and destroys the other.

Here, it seems, is naked assertion of the ego which conceals the tone of "For mine own good all causes shall give way," but the sophisticated articulation which has recourse to buts, ifs, and perchances, softens the violence to an extent.

Thoreau's social obligation does not go far; it is negative. First: not to be so unjust as to "wrest the plank" from a drowning man; he would rather drown himself; and then, which is fair, but not particularly noble or magnanimous, that he would simply wish to refuse allegiance to the State, to withdraw and stand aloof from it effectively. Nay, he is even prepared to do something more: "I quickly declare war with the State." That would have been edifying but for the qualifying clause which follows: "though I will still make what use and what advantage of her I can, as is usual in such cases." Here is an instance not of the State exploiting the individual, but *vice-versa*.

Notice here the parallel to Thoreau in Gandhi's earlier public life in South Africa. While he must have known that the Boers had a just cause Gandhi still advocated co-operation with the British Empire. He considered it his duty as a subject of the Empire to be loyal to the government; and even thought it unjust for every man to think he could criticize the government. It is well-known that he volunteered his services to tend the sick in the British army during the Boer War. Is it because his political sense had not been quickened sufficiently? Or is it because centuries of subjection had made even the best of us in India loyal to the government? Or is it, one is constrained to ask, expediency that prompted him to co-operate with the government and win its goodwill for India and Indians in South Africa? If so, this was reprehensible in one like Gandhi. In this respect despite what he said, Thoreau emerges nobler in action, for he thought it a "disgrace" to co-operate with a government – his own, here – which was waging an unjust war with Mexico and kept slaves. He denounced Massachusetts for letting her soul "trail in dirt." And he even pleaded passionately, poetically and yet without the remotest suspicion of pathetic fallacy:

> All nature would be affected and the sun's brightness fade, and the winds would sigh humanely, and the clouds rain and the woods shed their tears and put on mourning in midsummer if any man for a just cause grieve.

He could be more business-like, in the manner of Gandhi, a practical idealist.

> I know this well, that if one thousand, one hundred, if ten men whom I could name – if ten honest men only – ay, *if* one honest man in the State of Massachusetts, ceasing to hold slaves were actually to withdraw from this co-partnership, and be locked up in the country jail, it would be the abolition of slavery in America.

But, if reports be true, what happened is not particularly edifying. He did go to prison for his disobedience, spent one night and came out of it, thanks to the intervention of an aunt who paid the tax for him. Now, here is something which Gandhi would not have let anyone do. For it matters little whether you pay or your aunt pays.

These inconsistencies and contradictions are not infrequent in Thoreau though they are less frequent than in Gandhi, but Thoreau did not have to wage a daily war with authority. However, Gandhi did admit his contradictions and considered them a sign of growth in one who was experimenting with truth, and he clarified to the public that in case of inconsistency his later position on any issue must be taken as final. Thoreau offered no such defence. Indeed he justified it as inevitable when one is acting from principle – "action from principle" "not only divides families, ay, it divides the individual separating the diabolical in him from the divine."

It is possible that the New England Puritan background made for some sort of self-righteousness and even haughtiness in Thoreau. But largely it was the commercial values which dominated New England thinking that must have made him want to dissociate himself from those values and save at least himself from damnation. The American assertion of the ego which expressed itself on the physical plane in the extension of the frontier, manifested itself in his case as an attempt at acquisition of a new dimension, the extension of the inner frontier, the enrichment of the life of the mind and the soul – which must be considered rare and unique in the American context. Essentially it was a preoccupation with the self, though in rare cases like Thoreau's, the preoccupation was with the transcendental self. The net result however makes for a minimal, not maximal, discharge of one's social obligations as can be seen in his remark: "I cannot expect like Orpheus to change the nature of the rocks and trees and beasts." He would at best take care to keep *himself* free from taint: "If a man is thought-free, fancy-free, imagination free, unwise rulers cannot fatally interrupt him."

Toqueville, that classic commentator of the American scene, who is said to have invented the word individualism, observed that "individualism saps the virtues of public life and then is absorbed into the egoistic." He noted that while "egotism is as old as the world, individualism is of democratic origin"; that was Toqueville's fear for the future of American democracy. Recent political thinkers have demonstrated in their own thinking how Toqueville's fears have come true.

It is good to be aware that there is a tradition of duty in Western religious and philosophical thinking. The Calvinists for instance insisted that all that is not duty is sin. The Positivist School of August Comte pointed out that the individual had no rights but only duties – the right to do his duty. But neither of these has entered the mainstream of Western life; they are not part of the living tradition of the West. Not even Plato despite the ceaseless academic claim for the impact of Hellenism on Western thinking, for Plato tells us in his *Republic* that the mass of mankind are groping in a dark cave and one man (that is, the creative minority) who sees the light of day goes back to the cave to draw the uncreative mass into the open. My contention is that these scattered religious and philosophical thoughts have not been translated into a "tradition of *action*." Even when translated into action, the farthest the man of thought has gone is presented in "Shall I at least set *my* lands in order?"

Now the entire life and work of Gandhi is a repudiation of the individualism of the West and simultaneously a rejection of the Western as well as the Russian kind of Socialism, for he aspired after the freedom to build, in his own words, "a staircase to Sirius"—he anticipated the American astronauts so long ago. This man of God said so unequivocally that he was "endeavouring to see God through the service of humanity for I know (he said) that God is neither in heaven nor down below but in everyone." Hence his mission to "wipe every tear from every eye." Even his day of silence was a day of intense activity; and his prayer meetings ended with discourses on social issues. "Anything," he said, "which I cannot share with the masses is taboo to me." Hence also his declaration that he didn't wish to be reborn but if he did he would wish to be born as an untouchable to share their sorrows. Elsewhere he said with a conviction whose sincerity is unmistakable: "Suffering is the mark of the human tribe. It is an eternal law. The mother suffers so that her child may live. . . . The condition of wheat growing is that the seed grain should perish." From the natural law Gandhi turns to history for support: "No country has ever risen without being purified through the fire of suffering . . . the purer the suffering the greater the progress."*

This profound social concern of Gandhi issues from the immemorial Indian tradition, which has unceasingly advocated self-realization in and through society. Gandhi repeats times without

---

* The Vaishnava tradition which nourished Gandhi has its foundations in legends like the following which abound in Tamil literature: Ramanuja, the great exponent of Vaishnavism, was one day being taken in procession. At the head of the procession were his two great disciples, Dasarathi and Kuresa. On sighting a ***chandala*** woman Dasarathi felt perturbed and shouted to her to get away quickly lest her presence should pollute the great Master. And the woman whined: "Where shall I go? To my right is the God Sri Ranganatha, to my left is the river Cauvery, in my front is the Master and behind are the mansions of the great disciples; above is the sky, and the earth below does not claim me yet." At this Kuresa, the other disciple, felt a sense of shame and bid his companion, as Brahmin, to subject *himself* to *prayaschitta* (expiation) rather than cause hurt to the unfortunate woman. The essence of this ritual is in the suffering one inflicts on oneself in penitence.

number the ancient Indian doctrine: that for the good of the family an individual may be sacrificed, and a family in the interest of the village and a whole village for the good of the country. Which calls for narrow loyalties – loyalty to oneself is indisputably a narrow one – to make room for larger ones. "An individual's success," thought Gandhi, "will be like a millionaire's donating free food to millions of starving people." In Gandhi's scheme, and generally in the Indian scheme of things, neither is the society domineering nor does the individual feel the need to *assert*. Neither, because both individual and society recognize a higher law than both. Neither feels the necessity to push the other to an extremity with the result a spirit of accommodation has become the pervasive principle of life. Without such accommodativeness, there clearly could not have been a long line of most distinguished individuals throughout India's history, but their greatness is invariably in proportion to their capacity not to exalt the self, indeed to deny it. Her leaders have invariably been men of the spirit. Here is no Bill of Rights or the Rights of Man. Nor is there the Divine Right of Kingship. But if the king was sometimes looked upon by his people as God's deputy, the *Arthasastra* records that "The king on receiving the royal authority from the people's hands at the time of coronation had to take the oath: 'may I be deprived of heaven, of life, and of offspring if I oppress you'." For in the happiness of his subjects lies his happiness; in their welfare his welfare. It is interesting that in a popular version of the *Ramayana*, Kusa and Lava raise the question if the king had no right of his own when the people indulged in gossip about his wife's character. Apparently not. But by suffering Sita became the mother of the race. There may be hundred Ramas, said Vivekananda in one of his American speeches, but there is only one Sita.

Yet there the nightingale
Filled all the desert with inviolable voice.

It is possible to look at the epic as woven round an abducted woman as the *Iliad* is around Helen, but the two are at opposite ends – the one at the giving and the other at the receiving end.

Interesting that in our own time Motilal's son, Harrow- and Cambridge-educated Jawaharlal Nehru, when still in his twenties, on seeing the plight of the kisans in U.P., said to himself: it is better to be accursed with those unfortunate people than be saved alone.

Now what one misses not merely in Thoreau but in all the three writers we are preoccupied with is: their desire for action is not in commensurate with the intensity of their thought – there is, if one may look upon W.B. Yeats's distinction as still valid, a dichotomy, certainly a discrepancy between "perfection of the work" and "perfection of the life." Perfection of life is a misnomer according to the Indian tradition without social and metaphysical obligations – and the reason why action, disinterested action, becomes the central sustaining principle of the universe according to the *Bhagavad Gita*. If I cease to act for one split second, the universe goes to pieces, says Krishna to Arjuna. The Indian gods themselves took birth after birth for the good of the world. In myth, legend and epic, exceptional individuals have given their life so that others may live. Curiously, action has invariably accompanied suffering and sacrifice of the self, and since that is disinterested action it has led to vindication of the truth. Is that why Gandhi claimed that "the Rishis who discovered the law of non-violence were greater geniuses than Newton . . . greater warriors than Wellington"? Thus Bhagiratha brought the Ganga down the plains, Dadhichi gave his backbone to the gods to smite the relentless clouds with and bring rain to parched earth; thus Dasaratha sent his son to the forest and Rama himself banished Sita in obedience to the people's wishes. Thus Savitri decided to marry Satyavan in the full knowledge he was destined not to last beyond a year after her marriage, and Harishchandra sold his wife and child, and himself was in the employ of the lowest of the low; so did the child Prahlad drink poison. So did Nachiketa and Ekalavya bear suffering at their tender age to come out of the fire purer and stronger for the suffering – suffering is action, action suffering. Not merely in the Upanishads, legends and epics but in history too: the Buddha who spoke not of God, did nevertheless ask Ananda not to cross the threshold of this life even if he saw one human being in distress. He sounds as though he felt the *dukkha* of this world in his entrails. It is for the same reason that H.G. Wells considered the great victors of the Western world mere incendiary schoolboys in comparison with Ashoka. Whatever the impact of these myths on the "lost generation" of western-educated intellectuals at one time, we have now been reassured by psychologists and anthropologists of the West of the value of a national myth as the shaping spirit in the life of a people. All one has to do is to tap the national myth and release the psychic energy.

If a country's myths are the finest expressions of its collective unconscious, their significance is too profound to be minimized – only callow teenagers will do so today after the work of Frazer and Jung. One would go so far as to say: if you have no myth you must invent one. This country did not have to invent any, what with its magnificent mythical imagination. What Gandhi did was to invoke that imagination, to tap those hidden reservoirs of psychic energy and make them flow in our veins. Each people must fulfil their destiny in terms of their *swadharma*, an inner principle (would Hopkins's "inscape" be an adequate equivalent?) by which, for example, the oyster receives the rain from abroad, goes down to the bottom of the sea and diligently shapes the pearl – now, the pearl, is it the gift of the rain? of the sea? of the incessant inner industry of the oyster? The questions answer themselves.

It is not for nothing that on the assassination of Gandhi the *London Times*, not known to be very friendly to Gandhi or Hinduism, brought out a fitting editorial to say that no country but India and no religion but Hinduism could have produced a Gandhi; not for nothing did Professor Arnold Toynbee, the distinguished historian, write: Gandhi is not only India's benefactor but England's benefactor too, he civilized us; and Stanley Jones, the American Christian missionary could say that Gandhi converted him to his own faith. But millions of Indians, educated Indians, have only been at the receiving end in relation to Western thought, while a man like Gandhi, because he could respond from the deep well of India's wisdom, he alone could travel farther than did the millions and enrich mankind's heritage – and enrich even those from whom he received the stimulus. Here is the paradox of an essentially contemplative culture throwing up a saintly leader who could teach action to the action-oriented West.

The Swan-Maiden Myth and Dinkar's *Urvashi*

G.R. TANEJA

The widely known swan-maiden myths date from antiquity. In some form or the other, but with their basic features unaltered, they are found in varied cultural traditions all over the world. In the classical tradition, these myths appear in the form of the Cyenus myths, in the story of Leda and the swan, and in the symbolic mention of the birds with Apollo, the Muses, and Aphrodite. In the Slavic tradition, there is the Polish fairy tale of the Prince and the twelve geese princesses. Bulgarian Samodivas and Serbian Viles resemble swan-maidens. Then there is the Russian tale of "Sweet Mikhalilo Ivanovitch, the Rover, and Maryana, the White Swan." There are traces of this myth in the old Celtic tradition in "Dream of Oengus," and highly elaborate swan-maiden tales in the Teutonic literary tradition.

These myths have been variously interpreted. They have been treated as nature myths, the swan-maiden being the white cloud pursued by her captor, the swan-spirit. Others have considered swan-maidens and swan-knights as denizens of the world of the dead as well as symbolizing the founders of clans. Yet others have interpreted them as suggesting marital taboos among primitive people.[1]

In the Hindu tradition, the swan-maiden myth takes the form of the myth of Urvashi and Pururava. Urvashi is the only celestial nymph to be named individually in the *Rig Veda* where in a hymn she engages in a dialogue with her earthly spouse, Pururava, whom she has forsaken. She says:

> What am I now to do with this thy saying?
> I have gone from thee like the first of the Mornings.
> Pururavas, return thou to thy dwelling.

I, like the wind, am difficult to capture....
Thrice in the day did though embrace thy consort,
Though coldly she received thy fond caresses.
To thy desires, Pururavas, I yielded.
So wast thou king, O hero! of my body....
When loving these immortal ones, the mortal hath
Converse with the nymphs as they allow him.
Like swans they show the beauties of their bodies,
Like horses in their play they bite and nibble....
Nay, do not die, Pururavas, nor vanish: let not
The evil-omened wolves devour thee.
With women there can be no lasting friendship;
Hearts of hyenas are the hearts of women.[2]

Later, in the *Shatpatha Brahmana*,[3] the legend is described in greater detail. Urvashi, the nymph, loves Pururava, a king of the "lunar" race. She agrees to marry him on condition that she must never see him naked. The supernatural beings in heaven, who desire the return of their former playmate, play a trick. The condition of Urvashi's stay on earth is violated. She vanishes. Distraught, Pururava seeks her everywhere and eventually finds her and her companions swimming in the lotus-lake in the form of birds. They appear to him in human form. To his entreaties, Urvashi replies: "I have passed away like the first of dawn, difficult to catch." Though later she relents and the couple are united.

But for a later Vedic version, in which Urvashi agrees for a night's stay with the king, the tale remained an essentially tragic one with an unhappy ending, till Kalidasa rewrote it as a play called *Vikramorvashiyam* (*Urvashi Won with Valour*) and gave it a happy ending.

Though presented once again as the courtesan of Gods, Kalidasa's Urvashi is conceived in different terms. The essential features of the tale remain unchanged, but Kalidasa's Urvashi reacts with human feelings. She is shown capable of experiencing such human emotions as jealousy, frustration and disappointment. As a woman of infinite charm, she enchants her human lover. Yet she loves him deeply and pines for him in his absence. His indifference, even when it is for the briefest moment, pains her. She is jealous when the king but throws a fleeting glance towards another woman. The fickle, wanton whore of the Vedic lore emerges, in Kalidasa's play, as utterly human and poignantly vulnerable.

Tagore's "Urvashi,"[4] on the other hand, is more akin to Shelley's Intellectual Beauty.[5] Tagore calls her "the symbol of feminine beauty,"[6] the eternal woman whom man has always desired but never possessed. He depicts her arising, naked and flawless, out of the foam of primal ocean as it was churned by gods:

> White as the kunda-blossom, a naked beauty, adored by the king
> of gods
> Thou stainless One. . . .
>
> Wast thou never bud, never maiden of tender years,
> O eternally youthful Urbasi?
>
> Sitting alone under whose dark roof
> Didst thou know childhood's play, toying with gems and pearls?
>
> At whose side in some chamber lit with the flashing of gems,
> A smile on thy pure face?
> That moment when thou awakedst into the universe
> Thou was famed of youth,
> In full blown beauty!
> In the assembly of gods when thou dancest in ecstasy of joy,
> O swaying wave, Urbasi!
> The companies of billows in mid-ocean swell and dance beat on
> beat;
> In the crests of the corn the skirts of the earth tremble;
> From thy necklace stars fall off in the sky;
> Suddenly in the breast of man heart forgets itself,
> The blood dances!
> Suddenly in the horizon thy zone bursts asunder;
> Ah wild in abandonement![7]

Elsewhere Tagore has written about Urvashi: "She is just a woman--neither a mother, nor a daughter, nor a wife--she is beyond all family ties; she is the Enchantress."[8]

While Tagore's Urvashi is a concretization of an abstract concept, Sri Aurobindo's longer poem on Urvashi[9] depicts her in the tradition of Kalidasa. Her earthly attributes are still more pronounced, and her heavenly inheritance is now a mere shadow. Sri Aurobindo hails her as "Mystery! golden wonder!/Moving enchantress!" but her essential attributes are human and romantic:

> Paradise
> breathed from her limbs and tresses wonderful
> with odours and with dreams.[10]

The emotions that fill her heart at thé sight of her earthly paramour are those of love shot through sensually, and her own reaction to the fact of her being in love is marked by its earthiness:

> glad, not as of old
> A careless beam; for an august constraint,
> Unfelt before ruled her extravagant grace
> And wayward beauty; and familiar things
> Grew strange to her, and to her eyes came mists
> of mortal vision. . . .
> There was a happy trouble in her ways
> and movements; her felicitous lashes dropped
> with a burden.[11]

Urvashi's alienation from the celestial world, and her humanization are clearly emphasized here. Wandering in the hills where the lovers had sought repose, Urvashi addresses her paramour thus:

> How long shall we in woods, Pururava,
> Waste the glad days of cheerful human life?
> What pleasure is in soulless woods and caves?
> But I would go into the homes of men,
> Hear great sound of cities, watch the eager
> Faces tending to trade and mart and talk

With the bright girls of the earth, and kiss the eyes
Of little children, feel smooth floors of stone
Under my feet and the restraints of walls,
And eat earth's food from vessels made and drink
Earth's water cool from jars know all joy
And labour of that busy and brittle world.[12]

Aurobindo celebrates her newly acquired role of a wife:

sweet service
And household talks making her beautiful,
And trivial daily words and kisses kind,
And all the meaning dear of wife and home.[13]

The earth is glorified. The cold superiority of the Eternal Arcadia is downgraded. Sensual love and sweet bondage between man and woman is unique and is to be preferred to divine, whimsical sport of love. Pururava himself marvels at his later inclinations:

Men said of me: "The king Pururava
Grows more than man; he lifts to azure heaven
In vast equality his spirit sublime,"
Why sink I now towards attractive earth?[14]

The adjective reveals where the poet's own preferences lie. The same preference for the earth is expressed when, later, Tilottama addresses the king:

O king, O mortal mightier than Gods!
For Gods change not their strength, but are of old
And as of old, and man, though less than these,
May yet proceed to greater heights, self-evolved.[15]

Dinkar's long and meandering five-thousand-word preface to his poem offers no elucidation of its meaning. In the preface,[16] Dinkar observes that Urvashi is a symbol of intense longing, inextinguishable desire and insatiable lust. The lovers symbolize common humanity. Dinkar believes that if one way to escape from the spatial and temporal bondage, into which everyman is born, is through *yoga*, the other is through the fusion of the male with the female, the union of physical and spiritual planes.

Also, observes Dinkar in the preface to the poem, the physical union between them is yet insufficient. They still remain discontent. There is a power – Dinkar uses the word Shakti – that inspires them to seek each other and immerse their separate selves into one self and achieve a mystical union. The same power provokes them to strive towards a higher goal which is beyond their reach singly but which is attainable to both of them through each other. Pururava represents man's intense desire to leave the tangible world behind and attain the unearthly, aworldly plane of existence.

Here the poem and the poet disagree. In *Urvashi*, Pururava is presented as a discontented earthling moved by divine inspiration to seek a higher plane of existence. And yet, the poem also states, that Pururava considers Urvashi an obstacle in the way of his desire to respond to the call of the celestial world to perform higher deeds. In the poem it is made unmistakably clear that Pururava's desire to possess Urvashi is not integral to his wish to attain the unearthly plane of existence. He appears to cherish no goal which he considers attainable through his union with Urvashi and which is located beyond this union at a higher plane. For Pururava it is apparently a question of either-or. He, at first, seeks no other supernal attainment through Urvashi than the celestial damsel herself. Later the higher world urges him to free himself from the bondage to his passion for the nymph.

The paradox in Urvashi is that if Pururava, himself a mortal, seeks the celestial world, then Urvashi, the celestial inhabitant, seeks a life on earth. More so, in the poem, Urvashi's seeking after the earth is allowed to be fulfilled, while Pururava's wish to reach the irreachable heaven is shown to be hollow and unworthy of the mightiest inhabitant of the earth.

What the poem, in fact, offers us is a glorious defence of the earth's earthiness, the ripe and sensuous tangibility of the mortal world, as opposed to the airy nothingness of the eternal heaven. And here Dinkar takes his cue from Kalidasa. In act III of Kalidasa's play, Chitralekha, a companion of Urvashi, commends her to the care of the king lest she be reminded of the luxuries of heaven:

> When spring is vanished and the torrid heat
> Thickens, I must attend the glorious Sun.
> Do thou so act that this my Urvashi
> Left lonely with thee, shall not miss her Heaven![17]

Overhearing, the Jester, the king's companion, remarks:

> Why, what is there in Heaven to pine for? There
> You do not eat, you do not drink, only
> Stare like so many fishes in a row
> With wide unblinking eyes.[18]

What the Jester says in jest in Kalidasa's play becomes the central concern of Dinkar's poem. The very first canto establishes this dichotomy and the theme of the superiority of the earth is developed consistenly throughout the narrative.

The Nati and the Sutradhara, who act as the prologue to the poem, are conversing:

> The Heaven itself is wanting in fulness. If the earthborn wish to emancipate love from the bondage of touch, the sky yearns to embrace the beauty that the earth is. (7)[19]

> The passion that pulls the mortals heavenwards, draws irresitibly to the earth the beings of the heaven. (8)

The nymphs make nocturnal visits to the earth to drink deep the delights of nature and sing joyous song to celebrate the silvery nights. (8) One of the frequent celestial visitors to the earth, Menaka, strongly defends her love for the earth against Rambha's condemnation of the earth and its mortal denizens. Rambha believes that:

> The land of the dead is destined to nothingness; the world of angels is eternal. The gods are immortal, serene . . . their bodies like the pure, smokeless flames. The beauty of the earth is but transient. (10)

Menaka replies:

> The joys of the earth are denied in heaven. We of the skies being helpless, are but satisfied with mere shadows. We taste the pleasures of the earth by thinking or seeking; those of the earth alone drink deep its joys. (10)
>
> Like the fire that is fed with dried wood, man, though transient, yet lives most intensely. (11)

The handling of Rambha's defence of the celestial set up reveals quite explicitly of the poet's own bias. She is made to extol the superiority of the heavenly beings on the basis of the values which are in disgrace on the earth. She is shown to laud the nymphs's promiscuity and immoral conduct. She considers the earthly values of loyalty, motherhood and devotion meaningless. Throughout the poem, the glorification of heaven is allowed to be counterbalanced by the votaries of the joys of the earth. The unmatched devotion of the housewife to the home and hearth is upheld and the nymphs are condemned as divine whores.

In the third act in which Pururava and Urvashi finally meet and reveal their innermost thoughts to each other, the poet again tilts the scale in favour of the earth. Pururava's pride in his human destiny, his inveterate confidence, evident when he challenges the gods to war, and his deep devotion to the beautiful and the sensuous defined him as utterly human. Urvashi's reaction to and evaluation of the inner promptings that plague Pururava are presented in a manner which deepens the void and the emptiness that heaven represents.

The evolution of the myth of Urvashi shows an interesting development in a curious direction. It reveals Urvashi's gradual alienation from her heavenly origins to a fascination for the pleasures of the earth, leading to a willing acceptance of the fate of an earthling, and, finally, deliberate and reasoned rejection on her part of her celestial past. The early Vedic lore presents her as a courtesan, a divine whore, whose rigid pre-conditions to her union with Pururava render the myth a variation on Keats's "La Belle Dame Sans Merci." Urvashi's passion for her earthly lover is deeper and, in fact, more "human" in Kalidasa's play. Later, Tagore conceived Urvashi in entirely human terms. Sri Aurobindo likens her to a domesticated village girl. In Dinkar, finally, she opts for existence on earth as a result of deliberate choice. Her alienation from her celestial inheritance and her final, total humanization are complete in Dinkar. Her earliest mention in the *Rig Veda* delineates her sensuality embedded in her divinity – a curious combination of qualities that at once provokes desire and yet insists upon unapproachability. The poets down the centuries, it would appear, have gradually divested the nymph of her supernal connection to be able to locate in her person man's most cherished ideal of sensuality.

An examination of Dinkar's poetic output and his major concerns would reveal Dinkar as the least inclined to celebrate the coming of Urvashi as a dispensation of Divine grace on earth in the Vedic-Upanishadic terms, as his critics have sought to interpret *Urvashi*. Equally misleading are those critics who take their cue from Dinkar's preface to the poem and read meanings into his references to the Vedas, the Puranas, the Shakti Cult, Buddhism, Vaishnavism, or the Freudian-Lawrentian metaphysics of sex.

Urvashi is not without its faults. An absence of rapport between the professed intention of the poet and his achievement has already been discussed. The uneven treatment of the poem's various sections does not render it a unified whole. There are for that matter no signs of any architectonic design. The characters of Aushinary and Sukanya are fragmentary and have not been adequately developed. They lack the necessary artistic vitality to make them proper foils to their more significant counterparts in the poem. The narrative is jerky. The latter half is, as if, hurriedly brought to its end; nor is the denouement conceived imaginatively.

Even though Urvashi is presented duly supported by theatrical paraphernalia – five acts, the Sutradhar and the Nati, numerous stage directions and other theatrical devices--it remains much like Sri Aurobindo's longer poem *sans* the latter's "He said's."

An aspect of Dinkar studies which is likely to cause controversy is the influences that worked on the poet. Dinkar has written on Eliot, Tolstoy, and Shakespeare. In criticism he makes numerous references to Eliot, Leavis and Ezra Pound. He read D.H. Lawrence extensively and translated a number of his poems into Hindi (later published as *Atman ki Ankhen*, 1964). *Seepi aur Shankha* (1957) contains translation of poems by a number of poets including Ezra Pound. Some of the images, overworked by Lawrence, his obsessive concern with "blood" and "darkness," for instance, are repeatedly echoed in Urvashi. It is possible to trace many other images to Keats and Spenser. Three stanzas in act IV are a neat translation of Wordsworth's observations on the "child" in his "Ode to the Intimations of Immortality." But a wide familiarity with major English and European authors is common among educated Indians and random similarity of images or isolated examples of echoes of ideas does not prove that Dinkar was greatly influenced by any one of them in particular to a considerable extent, or some of the poets that he read at length, such as Lawrence, really became integral to his intellectual life.

As a tale of love between the human and the supernal, *Urvashi* immediately invites comparison with works such as *Endymion*, *Lamia*, and *Venus and Adonis*. A major concern in Keats's treatment of love between the human and the supernal is the tresspass--with its resultant consequences--that the human lover becomes guilty of. All these works have been interpreted for their allegorical meanings. *Endymion* has been interpreted as a "spiritual fable, the parable of the poetic soul in man seeking communion with the spirit of essential beauty in the world."[20] Pettet interpreted *Lamia* as embodying the idea "that love is an ultimately destructive force because its world is one of the illusion and unreality."[21] Dinkar's *Urvashi* does not lend itself to such allegorical interpretations without some violence. It is devoid of the tension and conflict that mark *Lamia* in particular. In the anthropomorphic world of *Urvashi*, the gods and the mortals co-exist on the same plane. The nature of the relationship of the Hindu gods and their mortal devotees cannot be explained by the fact, significant though it is, that in Hindu literature, as also, for instance, in *Urvashi*, the gods on the one hand are inclined to cherish and are capable of indulging in the earthly delights, and, on the other, the mortals have the virtues and the might of the angels and that the two worlds exist independently and yet are mutually open to each other. The explanation lies elsewhere. The Hindu mind is not capable of perceiving simultaneously the dialectical contrariety between the ephemeral, but warm and vital, life-sustaining ambience of the earth on the one hand, and the perpetual, but "deficient," heaven on the other. For them the one world is theirs now and the other hereafter. Hence the total absence of the multiple tensions in *Urvashi*, which, for instance, Keats is led to recognize in "The Ode on a Grecian Urn" and which arise chiefly out of his desire to reconcile the two irreconciliables; the warmth of love, beauty and life, even though ephemeral, and the cold permanence of art.[22]

NOTES

1. M.E. Seaton, "Swan-Maiden," *Encyclopaedia of Religion and Ethics*, ed. James Hastings (rpt. 1908; Edinburgh: T. & T. Clark, 1964).
2. *The Rig Veda*, trans. Ralph T.H. Griffith (Varanasi: The Chowkhamba Sanskrit Series Office, fifth ed., 1971), pp. 527-30.
3. See *Shatapatha Brahmana*, trans. J. Eggeling, xi, v, i in *Sacred Books of the East*, vol. 44.
4. Rabindranath Tagore, *Complete Poetry and Plays* (India: Macmillan, 1936), p. 123.
5. "[Tagore] was called, while still in his teens, the Bengali Shelley, and he has translated Shelley, and has acknowledged him as an influence. 'The Hymn to Intellectual Beauty,' he says, was like a transcript of his mind in his youth." Edward J. Thompson, *Rabindranath Tagore* (India: Macmillan, 1921), p. 54.
6. In a letter in Bengali dated February 1933.
7. The three stanzas quoted are translated from the Bengali original by Edward J. Thompson; see Rabindranath Tagore, pp. 55 and 57.
8. In a letter in Bengali dated February 1933.
9. *Collected Poems*, Sri Aurobindo Birth Centenary Library, vol. 5 (Pondicherry: Sri Aurobindo Ashram Trust, 1972), pp. 189-218.
10. *Ibid., Urvasie*, Canto I, p. 190.
11. *Ibid.*, Canto III, pp. 208-9.
12. *Ibid.*, Canto II, p. 198.
13 *Ibid.*, Canto III, p. 210.
14. *Ibid.*, Canto I, p. 191.
15. *Ibid.*, Canto I, p. 195.
16. Ramdhari Singh 'Dinkar' (1908-73), *Urvashi*, [Hindi] (1961; rpt. Patna: Chakraval Prakashan, 1973), pp. i-ix.
17. Kalidasa (c. 1000 B.C.), *Vikramorvashiyam*, trans. Sri Aurobindo, *Collected Plays*, vol vii, III, ii.
18. *Ibid.*

19. The quotations from the original Hindi are translated by the author.
20. Sidney Colvin, *Life of John Keats* (1957; rpt. Cambridge: Cambridge University Press, 1970), p. 123.
21. E.C. Pettet, *On the Poetry of Keats* (Cambridge: Cambridge University Press, 1957), p. 237.
22. Apart from the works that I have commented upon at some length, there are a number of other poems that draw upon the swan-maiden myth and may be referred to: "Urvashi" (Hindi, 1909) by Jayashankar Prasad (1889-1937); "Urvashi" (Bengali, 1929) by Bishnu De; "Urvashi" (Assamese) by Bimbeshwar Neog (1909-66); "Urvashi" (Assamese) by Jatin Duara. Urvashi the nymph appears in *Mahabharata*, too. She is shown passionately in love with Arjuna whom she is commanded by Lord Indra to teach good behaviour. Arjuna treats her as his mother and is cursed by the slighted nymph.

Index